A Practical Approach to
Parallel Computing

A Practical Approach to
Parallel Computing

S K Ghoshal

Universities Press

Universities Press (India) Limited

Registered Office
3-5-819 Hyderguda, Hyderabad 500 029 (A.P.), India

Distributed by
Orient Longman Limited

Registered Office
3-6-272 Himayatnagar, Hyderabad 500 029 (A.P.), India

Other Offices
Bangalore / Bhopal / Bhubaneshwar / Calcutta / Chandigarh
Chennai / Ernakulam / Guwahati / Hyderabad / Jaipur
Lucknow / Mumbai / New Delhi / Patna

© Universities Press (India) Limited 2000

First published 2000
ISBN 81 7371 132 1

Typeset by
OSDATA, Hyderabad 500 029

Printed in India by
Orion Printers, Hyderabad 500 004

Published by
Universities Press (India) Limited
3-5-819 Hyderguda, Hyderabad 500 029

Contents

Preface ix
List of Figures and Tables xi
1 Parallel computing 1
  1.1 Need for parallel computing 1
  1.2 Degree of parallelism 2
  1.3 Flynn's taxonomy 2
  1.4 Interconnection networks 4
    1.4.1 Dynamic interconnection networks 5
    1.4.2 Static interconnection networks 7
  1.5 Hypercubes 12
  1.6 Exercises 13
    1.6.1 Taxonomy 13
    1.6.2 Hypercubes 13
2 Shared memory and message passing 15
  2.1 Shared memory 15
  2.2 Message passing 18
  2.3 Programmability issues 22
  2.4 Exercises 23
3 Our own parallel computer 25
  3.1 Preamble 25
  3.2 Microprocessor 25
  3.3 Board-level architecture 26
  3.4 The operating system 27
  3.5 Programming language 28
  3.6 Guidelines for design 28
    3.6.1 Shared memory 29
    3.6.2 Message passing parallel computers 30
      Type of link 31
      Width of link 31
      Storage at each link 32
  3.7 Exercises 33
    3.7.1 Unix on PCs 33

3.7.2 BIOS	33
3.7.3 Memory map	33
4 The FIFO card	34
4.1 Block diagrams of the communication card	34
4.2 Details of communication card hardware organization	34
4.3 Architectural features of FIFO card	34
4.4 How to improve on this design	37
4.4.1 Mistakes that you should avoid	40
Write into remote FIFO	40
Use horizontal connectors	41
Use I/O mapped links and status port	41
4.4.2 New technologies you should use	41
Use EPLDs and FPGAs	42
Use a wider data-path	42
Put more links per card	42
4.5 Exercises	42
4.5.1 Decoder of an EPROM	42
4.5.2 Better link design	43
5 Putting it all together	44
5.1 Introduction	44
5.2 Hardware	45
5.2.1 Node-level architecture	45
5.2.2 Topology	45
5.3 Hierarchical design of system software	45
5.4 SERC multicomputing firmware	46
5.4.1 Initialization routines	46
Flushing	48
Repair	48
Setting the configuration	48
CMOS checksum	48
Re-invoking POST	49
5.4.2 Driver routines	49
5.4.3 Who uses the driver routines?	49
5.4.4 When does one have to change SERC firmware?	49
5.4.5 What the SERC firmware cannot do	49
5.5 High-level library for scalable distributed computing	50
5.5.1 Design considerations of the library	50
5.5.2 Specifications of the library	50
5.5.3 An epilogue to the library	50
5.6 Exercises	51
5.6.1 CMOS RAM	51
6 Programming aspects	52
6.1 Design of a parallel program	52
6.1.1 Efficient parallel programming techniques	53
6.2 How to make a bad parallel computer...	55
6.3 Routines facilitating parallel programming	56

6.3.1 Elementary routines	56
Symmetry among low-level routines	60
SERC firmware's counterpart of POST	60
6.3.2 Complex routines	61
Different approach	65
6.4 The E-cube routing scheme	65
6.5 Exercises	66
6.5.1 Routing messages	66
6.5.2 Relabelling hypercubes	66
7 Example applications	67
7.1 Dimension independent programs	67
7.2 The manybody problem	69
7.3 The Diophantine predicate satisfiability problem	71
7.4 The 2-D image recognition problem	72
7.5 Exercises	72
7.5.1 Developing application programs	72
7.5.2 Developing system programs	73
8 Case studies	74
8.1 How to get started	74
8.2 Some elementary programs	75
8.2.1 Fork and nodeid	75
8.2.2 Expression evaluation	76
8.2.3 Matrix addition	77
8.2.4 Matrix multiplication	79
8.2.5 Linear curve fit	80
8.2.6 Gaussian elimination	82
8.2.7 Simpson's 1/3rd rule	84
8.2.8 Filon's formula	85
8.3 Exercises	87
Bibliography	88
Index of terms	93

Preface

We need to educate ourselves and our students in parallel computing. For that we need:

- Good students, which we have
- Good teachers, which we must become
- Good textbooks, one of which I have tried to write
- An inexpensive parallel computer comprising
  - Hardware, which this book describes how to build on one's own
  - Good system software, which this book describes and explains how to implement
  - Scalable application software, which this book explains how to write on this machine as well as on other machines
- A group of experts in parallel computing as well as rich libraries of portable and useful parallel application programs which we will be able to cultivate once we have the above.

We Indians have always produced good application programmers for computers that the first-world countries have built. We must make sure that we produce the next generation of programmers for computers which will be highly parallel and distributed. This training must begin early and be comprehensive. For that we need hardware platforms. Unfortunately, parallel computers are very expensive. They are not easily available for the common student to write and run application programs on. None of these parallel computers can be mass-produced so as to make them affordable and common. None are so reliable as to serve the purpose of program developers at sites geographically remote from the research groups that developed them. Many universities and engineering colleges in India have introduced or are planning to introduce courses at both the undergraduate and postgraduate levels to teach issues in parallel computing. I have been in touch with them and have been working with them in different capacities. I have conducted or participated in a number of workshops in which I have taught using my parallel computer and the system and application software that run on it. I have tried to put in as much material as I can, in an organized manner, into this book, so that graduate and undergraduate level courses can be taught. You should read this book, read the other books mentioned in the bibliography and the books and documents that are relevant to you. Then, you must design and build your own parallel computer. How I did it is explained in this book. You have to do it in your own way. I have given a number of exercises at the end of each chapter that let you evaluate how competent you are in each of the skills that are required to design and build a parallel computer all by yourself. I am quite sure you will build a much better computer than I have and be enriched in the process with knowledge and experience that will serve you and your students for a whole lifetime. Even if you do not design and build your own parallel computer architecture, you may find it useful and convenient to use the technology that I have developed and described in this book. You will have different generations of PCs in your laboratory, all of which are not used all the time. You can interconnect them using the FIFO card described in this book and realize an inexpensive but efficient parallel computer. You can do your own research with this setup, as well as teach graduate and undergraduate courses.

This is how the book is organized:

- In Chapter 1, an introduction to parallel computing is given.

- This is followed by a survey of shared memory and message passing architectures in Chapter 2.

- Chapter 3 explains the practical aspects of designing parallel computer architecture in India and building a parallel computer.

- Chapter 4 describes the board-level architecture of the FIFO card.

- Chapter 5 explains how we put it all together to assemble a usable parallel computer.

- The low-level and high-level C-callable routines to program the parallel computer are discussed in Chapter 6.

- Some practical problems in advanced topics of research in Computer Science are solved in Chapter 7.

- How you too can solve your own problems of interest is explained in Chapter 8.

In order to make the best use of the book, you have to read up about the topics mentioned in the index at the end of the book from sources given in the bibliography.

If you are not interested in hardware, you can skip Chapters 3, 4 and 5.

List of Figures and Tables

1.1	A typical MIMD multiprocessor	3
1.2	A global memory multiprocessor	4
1.3	A two-bus interconnection	5
1.4	A crossbar interconnection	6
1.5	Multistage interconnection network	7
1.6	A linear array of 6 processors	8
1.7	A ring of 6 processors	8
1.8	A tree with 4 levels	9
1.9	A 9-processor star configuration	9
1.10	A 3×3 mesh	10
1.11	A 3×3 torus	10
1.12	Hypercubes of dimension 0, 1, 2 and 3	11
1.13	A hypercube of dimension 4	11
1.14	A hypercube can embed a mesh	12
1.15	A hypercube can embed a tree	13
1.16	Another illustration of a hypercube embedding a tree	13
2.1	Normal method of virtual address translation by the MMU	16
2.2	Virtual address translation scheme when shared memory is used	17
3.1	Memory map of the IBM PC with CGA adaptor	30
3.2	IDT7203 FIFO chip	32
4.1	Block diagram of communication card	35
4.2	FIFO link between two nodes	36
4.3	The card is enabled if either ROM or any link is addressed	36
4.4	The ROM is enabled if its range of address is decoded	36
4.5	Two PALs are used to decode	38

4.6	Interpretation of the status port	39
5.1	We match the PC at every level	45
7.1	A scalable program to compute π	69
8.1	Demonstration of forkall and nodeid	76
8.2	Expression evaluation	77
8.3	Matrix addition	79
8.4	Matrix multiplication body	80
8.5	First half of the curve-fit program	82
8.6	Second half of the curve-fit program	82
8.7	Triangularization	83
8.8	Back-substitution	84
8.9	Simpson's 1/3rd rule	85
8.10	Fourier integral by Filon's method	87

List of Tables

1.1	Hypercubes	12
4.1	Addresses of important modules on the FIFO Card	40
7.1	Speedups for different intervals for computing π	69
7.2	Speedups for the manybody problem	71
8.1	Time to execute forkall for different dimensions of hypercube	75

1
Parallel Computing

Chapter summary

Parallelism is introduced. Computer architectures are surveyed. Interconnection networks are described. Important topologies are explained.

1.1 Need for parallel computing

There is today an ever-increasing demand for high-performance and low-cost computers. Parallel computing has emerged as a major technology today to meet the present and future needs. This has resulted in the development of parallel architectures, parallel programming methodologies and problem solving techniques that work in parallel.

This book deals with these aspects of parallel computers. We first show you how you can build a parallel computer yourself from locally available components. Then, we show how you can effectively use this parallel computer. Coding efficient programs for practical parallel computers available today is not an easy task. Many factors have to be considered to write efficient and fast parallel programs. Some of the programming techniques discussed in this book are highlighted using different numerical programs. Some good programming practices have also been described and explained.

1.2 Degree of parallelism

For executing a program successfully, different numbers of processors may be required at different time periods. The total number of processors required to execute a program in each such time period is known as the degree of parallelism. An efficient parallel program has a high degree of parallelism.

Parallelism is of two types:

- Hardware parallelism
- Software parallelism

Hardware parallelism is built into the machine's architecture. Software parallelism is exploited by the concurrent execution of machine language instructions in a program as coded by a programmer or as generated by a high-level language compiler.

Parallelism can be attained by various ways. The two important ways of attaining parallelism are:

1. **Temporal / functional parallelism** In this form of parallelism a particular algorithm is broken up into many parts, and each break-up is executed by a different processor.

2. **Data parallelism** In this form of parallelism, the algorithm is not broken up, but the data set is. Each processor works with a part of the total data set. Engineering and scientific programs exhibit a high degree of parallelism due to data parallelism.

1.3 Flynn's taxonomy

Michael Flynn [1] introduced a classification of different computer architectures in 1972. The four different types of computer architectures are:

1. **Single instruction single data-stream (SISD) architecture** All sequential computers have the SISD architecture where a single instruction acts on a single set of data at a particular time.

2. **Multiple instruction single data-stream (MISD) architecture** In these computers, a multiple set of instructions act on a single set of data sequentially. Here, the same data set flows through a linear array of processors executing different instructions, for example, in the hardware implementation of systolic DSP algorithms [56]. In these computers,

the instructions act on a set of data in the CPU in such a way that the output of one instruction is fed as an input to the next instruction. When all the instructions are carried out, the final output is stored in the memory, instead of storing the output of each instruction in the main memory and reading it back to the CPU for the next instruction. This reduces the flow of traffic between the memory and the CPU, thus reducing the adverse effects [2] of the *von Neumann bottleneck*.

3 **Single instruction multiple data-stream (SIMD) architecture** A typical example of these computers are array processors. Here, a single instruction is carried out in parallel over a multiple set of data in different processing elements.

4 **Multiple instruction multiple data-stream (MIMD) architecture** In these computers, a set of instructions act on a multiple set of data in parallel. MIMD machines are termed multiprocessors or multicomputers. Multiprocessors are tightly coupled, while multicomputers are loosely coupled. In a tightly coupled system, the processors share memory and sometimes even the system clock. In these multiprocessor systems, communication usually takes place through the shared memory. In a loosely coupled system, the processors do not have a shared memory or a global clock. Each processor has its own local memory and local clock. The processors communicate with one another through various interconnection networks such as high speed buses. Such systems are usually referred to as distributed systems.

In a typical MIMD multiprocessor (Fig. 1.1) only one processor can access a particular memory at a particular time. Different processors can store

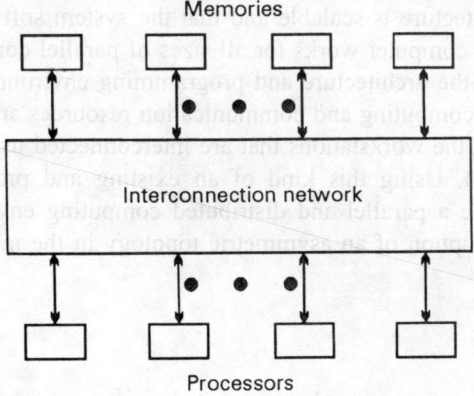

Fig. 1.1 *A typical MIMD multiprocessor*

in different memories simultaneously. A global memory multiprocessor is shown in Fig. 1.2. Here, P represents a processor and M a memory module. Each processor has its own local memory which can be accessed only by itself. The global memory can be accessed by all the processors. It stores only those data that are required by all the processors. This is because the global memory is neither fast nor large.

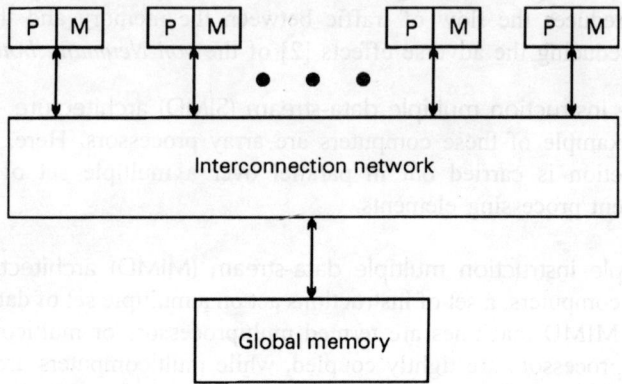

Fig. 1.2 *A global memory multiprocessor*

Multicomputers, on the other hand, have no global address space. They are loosely coupled systems. Each processor has exclusive access to its local memory. There has to be an explicit message passing between the processors whenever one CPU has to read what any other CPU has written. The processors can be connected to each other in different topologies. A topology can be either *symmetric* or *asymmetric*. In a symmetric topology, any given computing node can be logically viewed as the root node from where the execution of the parallel program is co-ordinated. Symmetric topologies with nice mathematical properties will ensure that the parallel computer architecture is scalable and that the system software developed for the parallel computer works for all sizes of parallel computers built in the lifetime of the architecture and programming environment. However, sometimes the computing and communication resources are unevenly distributed among the workstations that are interconnected using a local area network (LAN). Using this kind of an existing and practical configuration to realize a parallel and distributed computing environment often requires the adoption of an asymmetric topology in the model of parallel computation.

1.4 Interconnection networks

There are *static* and *dynamic* networks for connecting multiprocessors and multicomputers. These networks can be used for internal connection among processors, memory modules, and I/O disk arrays in a centralized system, or for distributed networking of multicomputer nodes. The topology of these networks can be either static or dynamic. Static networks are composed of point-to-point connections which do not change during the execution of a program. They are used for fixed connections among subsystems of a centralized system or among multiple computing nodes of a distributed system. Dynamic networks are implemented using switched channels, which can be switched on to match the communication demand of the program. Dynamic networks include buses, crossbar switches and Multistage Interconnection Networks (MIN).

1.4.1 Dynamic interconnection networks

A brief description of dynamic networks is given below.

1. **Bus** A bus is a collection of wires used for transferring data between processors, memory modules, and various other peripheral devices attached to the bus. Dynamic networks may include either a single-bus system or a multiple-bus system.

    (a) *Single bus* In a single-bus system, only one source (master) can be connected to one destination (slave) at a given time. Here the complexity in the number of connections is of order n, where n is the number of sources or destinations.

    (b) *Multiple bus* In a multiple-bus system, the number of independent source-destination connections that can exist at any given point of time depends on the number of buses. A two-bus system is shown in Fig. 1.3. Two different masters can be connected to two different slaves via the two different buses at the same time. The order of complexity of an m-bus system, with each bus interconnecting n nodes, is $m \times n$.

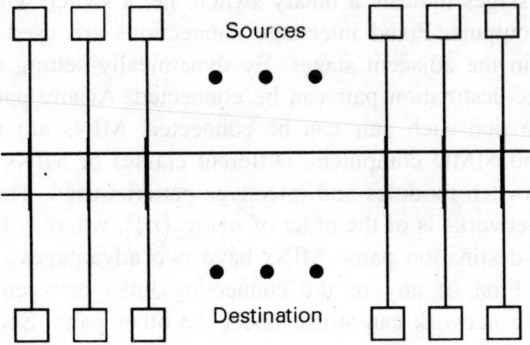

Fig. 1.3 *A two-bus interconnection*

2. **Crossbar switches** A crossbar switch network is shown in Fig. 1.4. It can be visualized as a single-stage switch network. Cross-point switches provide dynamic and independent connections between all possible source-destination pairs. Each cross-point switch provides a connecting path between a pair, which can be switched on or off depending upon the program's need. In this network, more than one source-destination pair can be connected simultaneously, but each slave can satisfy only one master's demand at a time. If there are n pairs, the maximum number of such independent connections at a particular time is n. In these networks, the complexity in the number of possible interconnection points is of the order n^2.

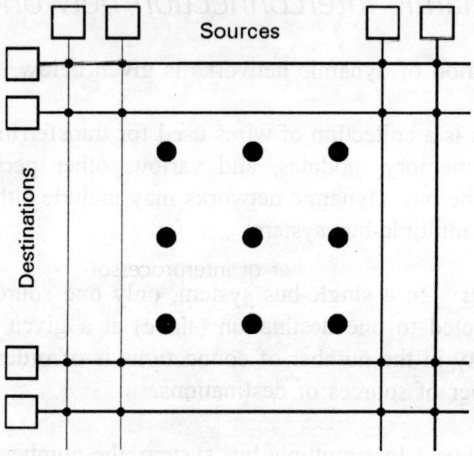

Fig. 1.4 *A crossbar interconnection*

3. **Multistage interconnection networks (MIN)** A generalized multistage interconnection network is illustrated in Fig. 1.5. Each of the boxes in the three stages indicate a binary switch, i.e, a switch with two inputs and two outputs. Fixed interstage connections are used between the switches in the adjacent stages. By dynamically setting the switches, any source-destination pair can be connected. At any particular time, more than one such pair can be connected. MINs are used in both MIMD and SIMD computers. Different classes of MINs differ in the types of switch modules and interstage patterns used. The complexity of these networks is of the order of $n(\log_2(n))$, where n is the number of source-destination pairs. MINs have two advantages over crossbar switches. First, if any of the connecting links between any pair is broken, the network can still connect the other pairs. Second, no two connecting paths overlap as in crossbar networks.

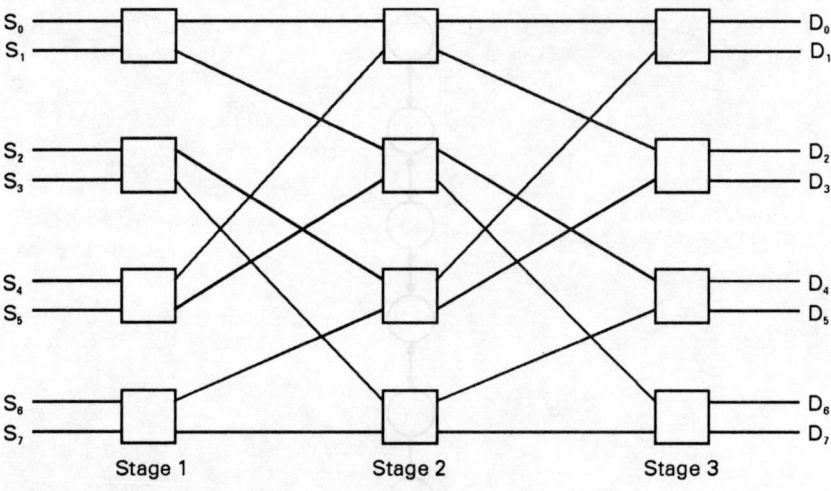

Fig. 1.5 *Multistage interconnection network*

Degree of a node

In a given topology, the number of interprocessor-communication links emanating out of a node is called its degree. The higher the *degree* of a node, the more difficult it is to physically build the machine because each link will require a number of wires. So many wires will have to go out of the node that it will become difficult to assemble the machine. It will also be more prone to failure of the links. On the other hand, the higher the degree of nodes in a topology, the richer it is in terms of interconnection resources and there are more possible paths between any two given nodes.

1.4.2 Static interconnection networks

Static interconnection networks use direct links which are fixed once they are built. Such networks are used to build multicomputers, where communication patterns are implementable using static connections. Thus, the implementations are cheaper, more scalable and practical. Some of the different topologies are:

1. **Linear array** It is the simplest connection topology (Fig. 1.6). It is a one-dimensional network where n nodes are connected linearly by $n - 1$ links. The terminal nodes have a degree of 1 and the internal nodes have a degree of 2, i.e, they are connected to two other nodes. This network is not very efficient in communicating for large values of n.

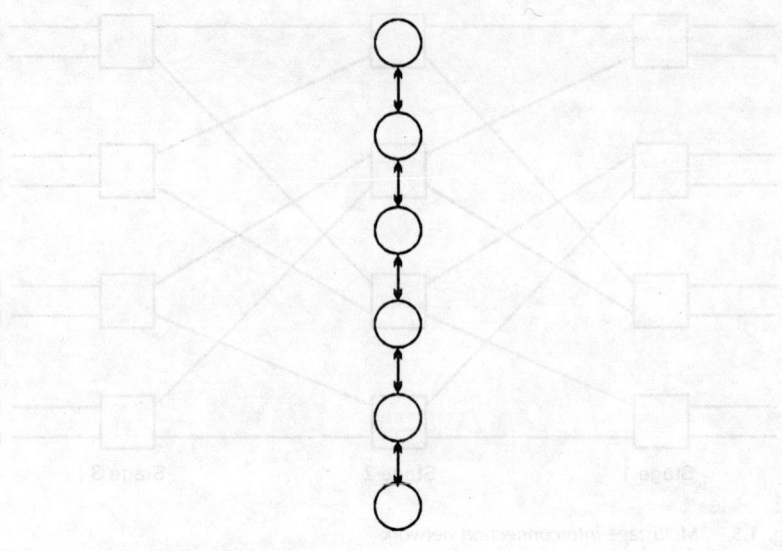

Fig. 1.6 *A linear array of 6 processors*

2. **Ring** A ring topology is shown in Fig. 1.7. The type of data-flow on the links in a ring can be unidirectional or bidirectional. It is a symmetric topology where each node has a degree of 2.

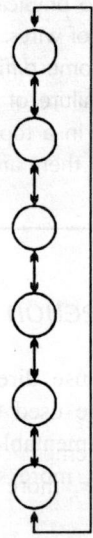

Fig. 1.7 *A ring of 6 processors*

3. **Tree** A binary tree topology with four levels is shown in Fig. 1.8. In general, a binary tree of k levels has $(2^k) - 1$ nodes. The degree of each node is at the most 3. With a constant node degree, the binary tree is a scalable architecture.

4. **Star** The star is a two-level tree as shown in Fig. 1.9. The star architecture is used in systems with a central supervisor node. The peripheral nodes are each of degree 1, while the supervisor node has a degree $n - 1$, n being the total number of nodes.

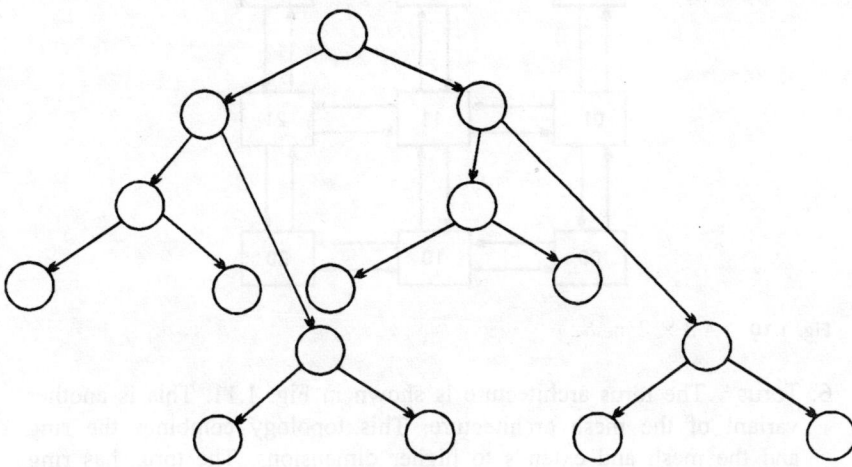

Fig. 1.8 A tree with 4 levels

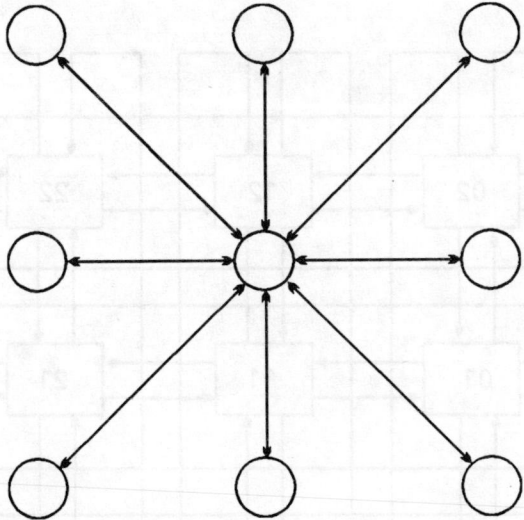

Fig. 1.9 A 9-processor star configuration

5. **Mesh** A 3×3 planar (or two-dimensional) mesh network is shown in Fig. 1.10. The Illiac IV, the DAP600 family of multiprocessors, the Thinking Machines CM-2 architecture, and the Intel Paragon have different variations of the mesh architecture [3]. In general, a k-dimensional mesh has n^k nodes, where n is the number of nodes in

each dimension, with each node having an internal node degree of $2k$. Dally's J-machine [4] is a three-dimensional mesh.

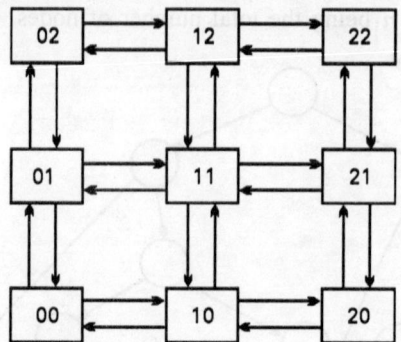

Fig. 1.10 *A 3×3 mesh*

6. **Torus** The torus architecture is shown in Fig. 1.11. This is another variant of the mesh architecture. This topology combines the ring and the mesh and extends to higher dimensions. The torus has ring connections along each row and along each column of the array. In general, a $n \times n$ binary torus has a node degree of 4. It is a symmetric topology.

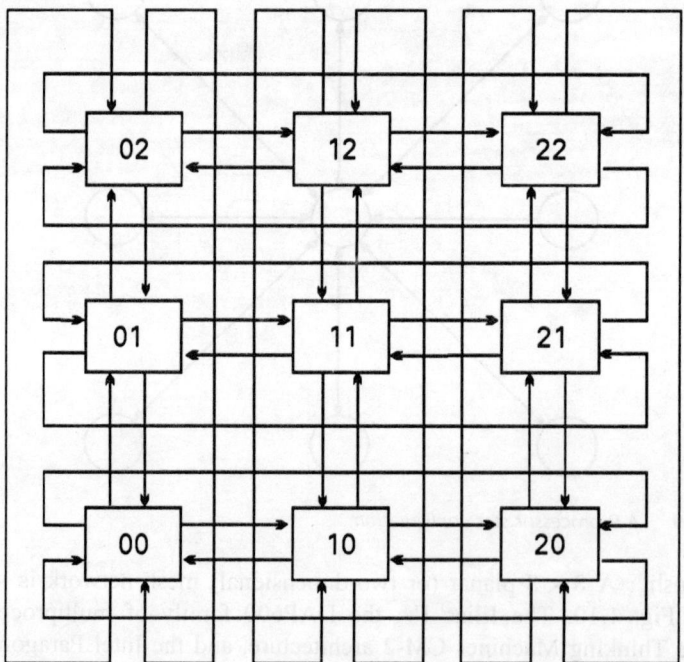

Fig. 1.11 *A 3×3 torus*

7. **Hypercube** The hypercube architecture can be of different dimensions. The dimension of a hypercube is the node-degree of each node. As the hypercube is a symmetric topology, the node-degree is the same for all nodes. Figure 1.12 illustrates the hypercube architecture for dimensions ranging from zero to three. Figure 1.13 shows a 4-dimensional hypercube. Table 1.1 illustrates the number of nodes or processors that are present in hypercubes of different dimensions.

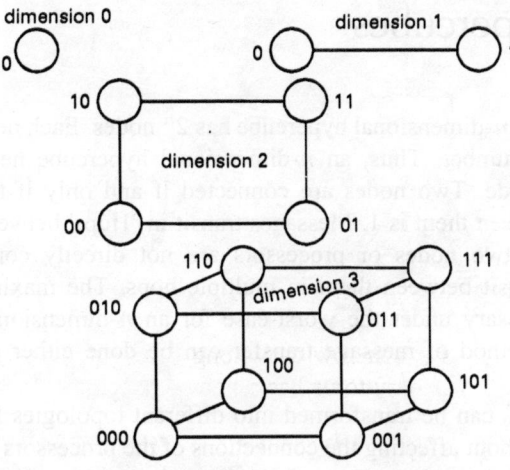

Fig. 1.12 Hypercubes of dimension 0, 1, 2 and 3

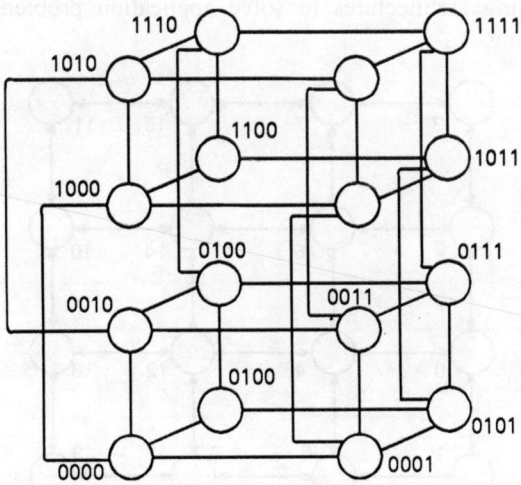

Fig. 1.13 A hypercube of dimension 4

12.   A Practical Approach to Parallel Computing

Table 1.1   *Hypercubes*

Dimension	Number of nodes
0	1
1	2
2	4
3	8
4	16

1.5 Hypercubes

In general, an n-dimensional hypercube has 2^n nodes. Each node is labelled as a binary number. Thus, an n-dimensional hypercube needs n bits to label each node. Two nodes are connected if and only if the Hamming distance between them is 1. Messages transit in 'Hops' between such node pairs. When two nodes or processors are not directly connected, then messages transit between them in multiple hops. The maximum number of hops necessary under the worst-case for an n-dimensional hypercube is n. This method of message transfer can be done either automatically or manually.

Hypercubes can be transformed into different topologies like the mesh or the tree without affecting the connections of the processors at each node. This is called *embedding*. Figure 1.14 shows how a hypercube can embed a mesh [57]. Figures 1.15 and 1.16 illustrate how a hypercube embeds a tree. Since the hypercube is a symmetric architecture, any processor can be taken as the root of the tree. Fox *et. al* [47] show how to use message-passing architectures to solve application problems in science and engineering.

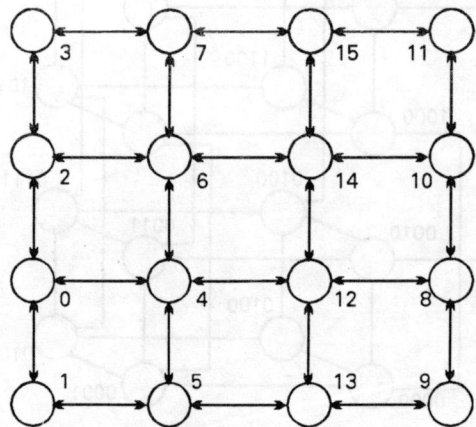

Fig. 1.14   *A hypercube can embed a mesh*

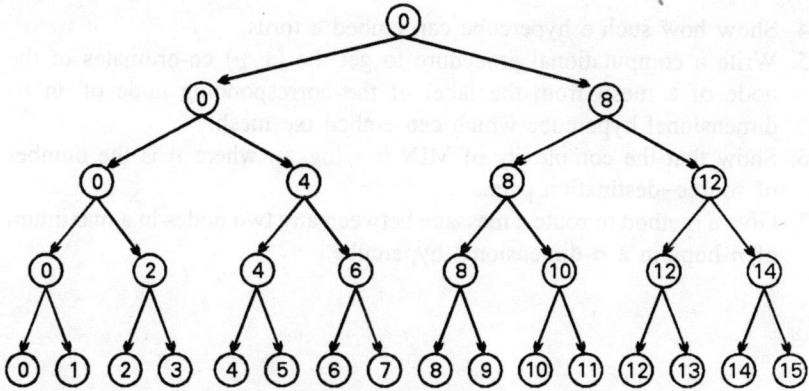

Fig. 1.15 A Hypercube can embed a tree

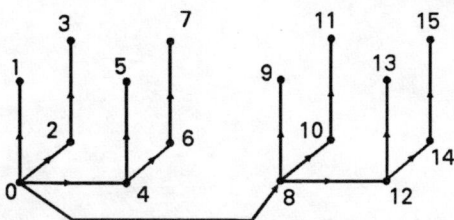

Fig. 1.16 Another illustration of a hypercube embedding a tree

1.6 Exercises

1.6.1 Taxonomy

1. How many computer architectures do you know of?
2. Classify all the computer architectures that you know using Flynn's taxonomy.
3. How many shared memory architectures do you know of? What are their CPU chips? How much memory can they share? Draw the block diagrams of these architectures. Do all shared memory locations in these architecture take the same time to access? Explain your answers.

1.6.2 Hypercubes

1. Draw a 6-dimensional hypercube and label each node.
2. Show how such a hypercube can embed a tree.
3. Show how such a hypercube can embed a mesh.

4. Show how such a hypercube can embed a torus.
5. Write a computational procedure to get the (x,y) co-ordinates of the node of a mesh from the label of the corresponding node of an n-dimensional hypercube which can embed the mesh.
6. Show that the complexity of MIN is $n\log_2 n$, where n is the number of source–destination pairs.
7. Give a method to route a message between any two nodes in a maximum of n-hops in a n-dimensional hypercube.

2
Shared Memory and Message Passing

Chapter summary

Two principal ways of integrating multiple CPU computers are compared and contrasted. Virtual address mapping and translation techniques are explained. Issues in programmability are highlighted.

2.1 Shared memory

Generally, shared memory machines are constructed by plugging in processor cards and memory boards into a backplane bus. Examples are the Multibus II [47] from Intel and VME [48] bus from Motorola. This allows a number of processors to share the memory. Architectures like those shown in Fig. 2.1 can thus be easily realized. The backplane bus is usually kept in a card-cage that also has a power supply and certain other modules that allow arbitration to take place for concurrent access requests, provide input/output operations, support DMA operations and different types of bus-access protocols, generate clock signals, provide reset signals, and synchronize different events all over the bus. The card-cage and the backplane also support locating and addressing the cards geographically (*i.e.*, indicating in which physical slots they are actually plugged in) and support diagnostics on power-up/reset or whenever required.

Too many cards cannot be plugged into the backplane bus. Cages come in sizes that typically hold 6 or 9 cards. The backplane bus too has a maximum length (about 18 inches) beyond which signals will get corrupted and/or reach too late to serve fast processors and memories. There also is a maximum number of bus masters (twenty for Multibus II) between whom access requests can be arbitrated. Having to arbitrate using a centralized mechanism results in a tremendous loss of throughput. This can be alleviated partly by using local memory buses like the Intel iLBX II local bus extension to the Multibus II [49], which allows the architecture to resemble Fig. 1.2.

Operating systems and compilers are written over this type of hardware. There is a way of using these machines which simply allocates disjoint tasks to distinct CPUs. Each CPU has it own local memory with which it interacts over the local bus. Thus, it ensures a high rate of throughput without the backplane bus becoming a bottleneck. Very coarse-grained task partitioning too can be efficiently supported at the operating system level using this approach.

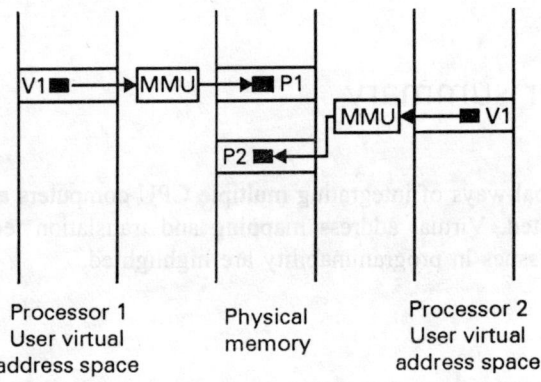

Fig. 2.1 *Normal method of virtual address translation by the MMU*

It is not difficult to write compilers that generate code which work correctly on shared memory machines. Compilers always produce codes that span the virtual address space of user processes. Operating systems initialize the Memory Management Units (MMUs) which translate these virtual addresses into physical memory addresses. When generating codes for modifying/accessing non-shared memory objects, typically placed on local memories, the MMU is initialized to translate as shown in Fig. 2.1. Even if two user virtual addresses are identical, the physical addresses produced for the two processors are distinct and disjoint; thus, unless the user program wants to share an object, it is not shared even if it has the same name as another object accessed by a program executing on another CPU.

On the other hand, when it is indeed intended to share an object between two (or more) CPUs, all one has to do is to program the MMU

Shared Memory and Message Passing   17

to work as shown in Fig. 2.2 and use the name of the object in the source codes of the programs that run on the CPUs. The object codes will reference the same user virtual address which the MMU will translate into the same physical address.

Thus, the compiler cannot and need not be concerned with the functioning of the MMU or its initialization. In fact, compilers are not even aware of the existence of an MMU. Compilers always produce object codes that work in the user virtual address space. This space is contiguous and typically as large as the size of the virtual address space of the CPU in question. It will be 4GB when there are 32 address bits of the CPU, and one can address anywhere within this space using a 32-bit pointer.

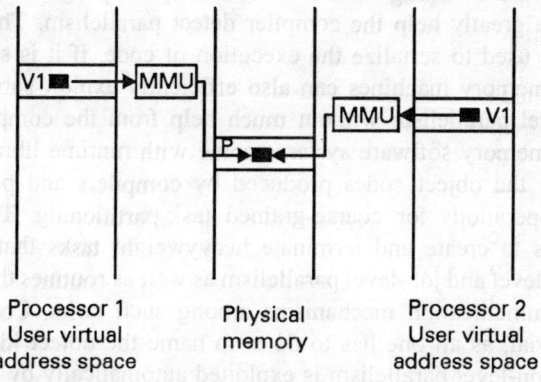

Processor 1   Physical   Processor 2
User virtual   memory   User virtual
address space   address space

Fig. 2.2 *Virtual address translation scheme when shared memory is used*

The physical address, on the other hand, varies from platform to platform and is normally discontiguous. That is true even for sequential platforms, as can be seen from Fig. 3.1. On a given shared memory parallel computer platform, apart from holes, there are shared memory segments that physically exist. There are segments of physical memory that are populated by memory-mapped devices which are plugged into the backplane to support secondary storage and/or Input/Output devices. Configurations vary widely between platforms and they change with time even on a given platform, as you add more processor boards and plug more memory cards into the backplane. The information about the configuration is usually kept in an area managed by the initialization firmware when the shared memory computer system is in operation. It is backed up in a non-volatile CMOS RAM which is powered by a battery. The CMOS RAM has a low drain current and the battery can power it for years. The MMU is programmed by the fiimware. Depending on the configuration, the MMUs at each processor are programmed so that valid regions in the user virtual space are mapped onto corresponding regions of the physical memories, both shared and non-shared types. Thus, not only the user application programs, but even Unix kernels can run on a variety of shared memory machines (belonging to a given genre) without their even having to be recompiled, let alone rewritten, so long as the proper initialization program is run. This is one great advantage of shared memory machines so far as developing and maintaining the software is concerned.

Whenever any write operation on an object is completed in a shared memory machine, all subsequent read operations will get the result of the modification, regardless of the identity and geographical location of the processor that wrote the object. This property makes it easier to generate codes automatically from high-level languages for shared memory machines and to run them on physical platforms. This also makes it possible to have very lightweight tasks capable of exploiting the fine-grained parallelism present in the program and detected by the compiler. Sometimes micro-tasking switches installed by the programmer within the source code greatly help the compiler detect parallelism. These switches can also be used to serialize the execution of code, if it is so desired.

Shared memory machines can also efficiently exploit subroutine-level and job-level parallelism without much help from the compiler. In fact, all shared memory software systems come with runtime libraries that are linked with the object codes produced by compilers and perform some primitive operations for coarse-grained task-partitioning. That is, there are routines to create and terminate heavyweight tasks that can exploit subroutine-level and job-level parallelism as well as routines that create and destroy communication mechanisms among such tasks. Communication itself is trivial, as all one has to do is to name the object identically.

Instruction-level parallelism is exploited automatically by the CPU and other board-level hardware. Shared memory multiprocessors do not come in the way of exploiting these types of parallelism. Thus, had they been scalable, shared memories would have been ideal for building parallel computers with and programming models that assume a uniform global user virtual address space all over the parallel computers would have been the ideal model to develop parallel algorithms and write compilers.

2.2 Message passing

Full-fledged computers interconnected by a communication network comprise a message-passing multicomputer. Each computer is complete. It has its own CPU, memory, I/O devices and peripherals. Each machine can execute its programs without having to refer to the network in any way, unless the programs explicitly address the network. The connection of the node to the network, or even the presence of the network does not in any way affect the execution of CPU-memory intensive programs executing on the nodes.

Any memory object can be private to a node or distributed over many nodes. If it is distributed, then each node accessing it in any way must have a copy of the object in its own local memory. If a node modifies its own copy of a distributed object, nothing happens to the other copies. If one desires that other copies be updated when a given copy is updated, it has to be explicitly arranged. Complex protocols, which do not always work correctly are necessary to update all copies of a distributed object. In cases where the communication network is slow and/or congested, shared data objects that are modified during the execution of a parallel program are often inconsistent. The only way to request that a given object be modified is to send a message to the node holding that particular copy of the object. The only way one node can send a message to any other node is to write the message into its own network interface. It cannot and does not know when the message will reach its destination or even whether it will reach at all. Any algorithm that assumes an upper bound on the time it will take for a message to reach, will fail to work correctly when implemented on a message-passing multicomputer with a large number of nodes. The time it takes for a message to reach may be small (i.e., comparable to the time it takes to modify the object in the node's own local memory) or very large. If it is very large, then only coarse-grained task-partitioning schemes can be efficiently implemented on such multicomputers. Algorithms for message-passing multicomputers should be so designed that the computations at each node should be able to go on as long as possible without depending on what is happening at the other nodes. Communications should be few and far between. Implementation of such algorithms on practical multicomputers should adopt certain clever techniques to compensate for the enormous delay in communication. Some of these techniques have been explained in Section 6.1.1.

Unlike shared memory multiprocessors, message-passing multicomputers can have large geographical distances between the nodes, and in a given network of such nodes there need not be any upper bound on the number of nodes. This makes it possible to build message-passing multicomputers with a very large number of nodes.

CISC and RISC

CISC and RISC are terminologies used to classify CPUs into two categories. The classification is somewhat subjective and the distinction is a bit hazy. RISC stands for "Reduced Instruction Set Computer". CISC stands for "Complex Instruction Set Computer". Note that these are misnomers, as it is the CPU that is being branded and not the entire computer. CISC CPUs allow many ways to get at an operand that resides in the memory. RISC CPUs allow only move-operations between a memory location and a CPU register. CISC instructions can have a variable length. RISC instructions always have a fixed length. CISC instructions can take a variable amount of time to complete execution. All RISC instructions take the same amount of time. Some CISC instructions can be very powerful.

All RISC instructions have the same strength. Instructions occur in a stream and the stream is compiled from a high-level language source code. All CPUs execute or at least try to execute more than one instruction from the stream simultaneously. This is known as *pipelining*. RISC CPUs allow better co-ordination [53] among instructions in the pipeline and this results in a better sharing of different resources within the CPU. This is because the compiler can predict which instruction will need which resource, at what stage of its execution and for how long. So RISC CPUs yield better performance. RISC is the modern trend of CPU design. There are many CPU vendors who brand their CPUs as RISCs, whereas actually they are not. Also, the intelligent reader may note that simply by being a RISC, a CPU does not guarantee higher performance on a given application. It all depends on how the high-level language code is compiled to take advantage of the CPU architecture. Thus, CISCs can be exploited by executing their powerful instructions, thereby at times outperforming a RISC. There is no reason for a vendor to feel defensive about the CPU being a CISC.

Interprocessor communication networks vary widely. Today, Ethernet, FDDI, serial communication links [52] and special-purpose communication links are all used with different degrees of usefulness in realizing working message-passing multicomputers. Even backplane buses have special-purpose communication hardware implemented as VLSI chips to facilitate message passing [50, 51]. Practically anything that can be used to make two computers interchange data, can also be used to build a message-passing multicomputer. After many generations of evolution, message-passing multicomputers, as they are built and used today, can be classified into two broad categories.

- Full-fledged workstations interconnected by large-delay communication networks. A typical example is a number of RISC workstations interconnected by Ethernet and FDDI. One cannot afford to have too many nodes. The network has other work to do apart from conveying messages related to a distributed computation in progress. These multicomputers are usually programmed by portable libraries like PVM [N_1, N_2] and MPI [N_3, N_4] which are freely available over the Internet or otherwise for those who need more computing power than what a single workstation can supply. End users need not always be interested in devising good algorithms for distributed memory computers or even in any other issue in parallel/distributed computing. They, however, are really the ones who take parallel computers seriously, make a lot of good use of them and are happy with whatever substandard system software and communication hardware they can have access to. They are the people for whom good parallel computers should be built and for whom good system software should be written. Any given computing establishment can be viewed as and/or converted into such a distributed computing environment. The hardware is already there. The system software can be easily procured. The applications can be written if one has the time and the patience. If you are writing application programs for these types of multicomputers, try to exploit only coarse-grained parallelism. Use the techniques that are explained in Section 6.1.1 to write efficient programs.

- Embedded microprocessors (each incorporated in a node-card comprising local memory, support chips that are needed to realize a single-board computer and a network interface that connects the node to a special-purpose network) are interconnected by a high-speed, high-bandwidth, special-purpose network which has been designed to support distributed memory parallel computation. These networks have many independent data paths which can work in parallel and through which messages can be very intelligently routed. Even though the number of nodes is very large, these networks try to deliver all messages as soon as possible. They try to ensure that no part of the network becomes too congested. They attempt to ensure guaranteed delivery of messages. Some of these networks even provide acknowledgments that messages have reached their destinations. Fault tolerance is built into some of these networks. With these networks, it is easier to maintain consistency of shared data objects. Relatively finer-grained task-partitioning schemes can be efficiently supported on these platforms. The only purpose of the node-cards/chips is to serve in parallel computers. Even when nobody is using the parallel computer, or that part of the parallel computer, no meaningful use can be made of the hardware by sequential application programs. The entire network of processors can serve only as the back-end processor of a workstation (usually running some kind of Unix) serving as a front-end. The back-end processor does not run any intelligent operating system capable of managing any kind of resources or capable of projecting any more sophisticated programmer's view than the bare hardware can. There really is not much of system software to manage the resource of the back-end, apart from what is linked with the object code produced by compiling the user programs by running a compiler on the front-end. See [55] for one such library of routines. There are many such environments, at least as many as there are multicomputers of this architecture. The system software for these types of multicomputers is invariably supplied by the hardware vendor and is priced. It is not available over the Internet or from an open source. It is usually very closely tied to the hardware platform. Software developed on these machines is not portable. There is no major incentive to develop software by a third party for these types of machines, particularly for commercial purposes, as nobody will buy the software unless he or she owns the same type of hardware platform. Vendors of such multicomputers have to either suffer a financial loss, or severely overprice the equipment, so as to minimize the loss. This is because these types of multicomputers do not sell in large numbers, for reasons explained earlier in this section. Therefore, these machines are not mass-produced. So, components of this kind of multicomputers lack quality control, and spare parts are difficult to procure and stockpile. That makes these machines unreliable and unfit for use by novices in a general-purpose computing environment. There are two types of organizations who own and use these types of multicomputers:

- Those who carry out message-passing multicomputing that is possible only with low-latency communication networks, as they use fine-grained and innovative task-partitioning schemes and scheduling strategies.

- Those who use parallel computers not because they need the results of the computation, but rather because they do research in certain issues in parallel computation that require them to use special interconnection networks to interconnect nodes.

Single-chip nodes for message-passing multicomputers

With the advent of VLSI technology, we can put a CPU, local memory, peripheral controllers (as required to realize a complete computer architecture) and message-passing communication links on a single silicon chip. The IMS T800 transputer [56] from Inmos is such a single-chip microcomputer specially designed for distributed memory parallel processing. It has, all integrated on one chip, a powerful 32-bit microprocessor, 4KB of RAM, four high-speed communication links, a floating point co-processor, programmable interval timers and an external memory interface.

2.3 Programmability issues

Shared memory machines are easier to program than distributed memory machines. This is because the moment one processor modifies a memory object, all other processors can see the result of the modification. In a distributed memory machine, if an object is modified in the virtual address space of a node, copies of the same object, residing in the virtual address of the other nodes are not affected in any way. It is the responsibility of the programmer to send copies of the modified object to other nodes. Or else, all other copies must be invalidated so that read accesses on any of the copies will result in the modified object being brought into the client node. If that is not done, read accesses will be made from stale copies and the parallel program will produce wrong results.

The updation/invalidation of copies of the same object over the nodes of a distributed memory parallel computer cannot be done in a scalable manner. For any distributed memory parallel computer, as the number of nodes increases, the time period for which the modified object remains in an inconsistent state increases. Different copies may hold different values for the same object. This is inevitable regardless of who has generated the code. Be it the application programmer by explicit command, the compiler-generated code on execution or the operating system as part of its routine chores that updated/invalidated the copies, too many copies just cannot remain consistent for too long a time. Shared memory machines have no such problem. But they cannot be built with a large number of nodes being able to access a shared memory object in constant time.

Shared memory machines always need synchronization. Otherwise, an object may be modified more than once without anyone being able to see the result of the first modification (write-after-write hazard). A client processer may read the object even before it was modified once (read-before-write hazard). To implement synchronization, there must be synchronization primitives in HLL, special lock instructions in the CPUs and arbiter hardware in the memories. These arbiters cannot scale. They cannot work properly when there are large propagation delays of signals. Thus, arbiters do not work over large geographical distances.

Implementing a shared memory programming model does not require physical memory to be shared between CPUs. It is enough to have local memory modules at each node, interconnected using static interconnection networks. But such implementations cannot ensure consistency and scalability simultaneously.

It is an art to develop programs that work in parallel on large distributed machines. The idea is not to have any centralized data object that has to be modified any time during the execution of the program, in such a way that many other CPUs have to see the modified object and act on its state. Some application programs lend themselves nicely to this requirement. Others require new algorithms to avoid centralized objects and newer techniques of implementation. All these are subjects of active research in which we shall be able to participate as long as we have our own parallel computer. The next chapter describes how we can build one.

2.4 Exercises

1. Compare and contrast between shared memory and message-passing architectures.

2. Is any form of parallel computing also some type of distributed computing? If so, why? If not, why not?
3. Name an application of distributed computing, where frequent updating operations have to be done on a shared object, and yet the nodes that do the updating must be spread over a wide geographical region.
4. Draw the bus-transaction timing diagram for a backplane bus with four CPUs sharing memory and contending for access to it.
5. What is the *Cache coherence problem*?
6. What is a snoopy cache?
7. Whenever any information moves from one place to another place in a parallel or distributed computer, what happens basically is that one group of flip-flops set/reset the state of another group of flip-flops over a number of transmission lines. Why is it then that shared memory machines always ensure that the result of the latest write operation is reflected in the values returned by subsequent reads, whereas in message-passing machines, no such guarantees can be given?
8. Can you think of a problem that is more suited for shared memory machines than for message-passing machines and vice-versa?

3
Our Own Parallel Computer

Chapter summary

Practical guidelines in the design of a parallel computer architecture are explained. The guidelines take into account a low budget, typical Indian educational/research environment. The guidelines cover CPU architecture, board-level architecture, operating systems, and programming languages. A message-passing model is chosen over a shared memory model. Architectural parameters are decided upon.

3.1 Preamble

Let us build a parallel computer, for our own use and for further research in different areas of parallel computing. In the process we will also learn many lessons in system integration of a parallel computer, hardware, system software, application programming and in being practical about these issues. Let us build it in such a way that, despite the limited availability of components and software and the limitations imposed by a very low budget and manpower, we still realize a practical, usable and efficient parallel computer.

3.2 Microprocessor

Let us use the Intel 80X86 series of microprocessors. They are inexpensive and easily available in India. Literature and documentation from Intel literature sales department [6] and many independent authors of articles in magazines [7] and textbooks [8,9,10] are available about these microprocessors. Same is the case with other supporting chips [11] needed to integrate a board-level architecture (of single-board computers) and different peripheral controller chips that go with these single-board computer architectures. It is easier to find people who have been developing board-level products featuring some of these chips. Expertise in developing board-level hardware products featuring other types of chips is relatively rare. Assemblers and high-level language compilers generating target codes for these microprocessors are readily available from Intel [12] and many third-party vendors [13]. Textbooks of assembly language programming are available as inexpensive Indian editions [14]. Experts of assembly language programming are around as personal computers are common and their architectural details are well known.

3.3 Board-level architecture

Let us choose the IBM PC [15] as the single-board computer architecture to serve as nodes. IBM PCs are widely available. Many vendors sell them at competitive prices. As months pass, the prices decrease. When any component of the IBM PC gets old and/or defunct, it can always be replaced with a newer generation component that works much faster and costs much less. The IBM PC architecture is open. It is adequately described in literature published by IBM [15,16]. As Intel announces advanced microprocessors in the 80X86 family, they are readily incorporated in single-board computers made by a large number of third-party hardware developers. Once a given design of motherboard has proved itself in the market, it is mass-produced and thus its price plummets. Different types of motherboards are available featuring the same CPU chip with varying clock speeds and size and type of memories. All these motherboards are software compatible with each other. Much literature is available [17] about the base-architecture of the motherboards and all the versions of BIOS [15,16,18] strive to project a uniform view of the hardware that they control. This is done by providing a BIOS-call interface that is common across all improvements that are done over the base architecture by different vendors. All types of information needed to work with the PC hardware [15,16,19], system software [20,21] and for interfacing the PC [6,8,11,15,16] with other digital hardware are freely available [22].

The real reason

Also think of the worst-case possibility. What happens if we cannot build a parallel computer and give up our effort after a finite amount of time?

Had we tried to build special-purpose board-level architectures to serve as the nodes of our parallel computer, we would have found no use at all for the abandoned single-board computers, as they need special purpose software for anything and everything. And so, for any use to be made of these boards, we would first have to develop the software and only then use it. That will be rather painful, particularly considering our state of mind caused by the failure in the first place. On the other hand, with IBM PC motherboards, if all else fails, we can always make personal computers out of the motherboards and use them as all the software is already available. Thus, we decided to use IBM PC as the node-level architecture of our parallel computer. However, do not worry. Our story will not have any such tragic ending. Not only shall we design, build, own and operate a real parallel computer that works efficiently and is easy to program, we will describe it in this book. We will also develop a way of using the nodes of our parallel computer individually as sequential PCs while they can, at the same time, be used to run tasks belonging to parallel computation. Thus, we will develop mechanisms to do practical and inexpensive distributed computing as well as a by-product of the technique we develop in this book. Our ability to use the PCs for distributed computing is an important benefit that derives from our early decision to use the IBM PC's board-level architecture. Another strength of our architecture — that it supports heterogeneous nodes comprised of IBM PCs of different processor types and on-board configurations — also derives out of this decision.

3.4 The operating system

At the time that I decided to build a parallel computer, MS-DOS [18,20,21] was the only operating system available on the PC platform. Even now, it is the most common operating system that runs on the PC. Program development tools, compilers and other utilities that one would use when developing the hardware and system software of a parallel computer were all available only on the MS-DOS platform. So, I chose MS-DOS to be the base operating system for the parallel computer. That was in 1987 and I did not then know enough about the internals of Unix. At that time the popular 8088 CPUs and the PC platforms they featured in, did not have the architectural support for Unix. Not many Unix versions were around for the PC platform when the PC architecture grew powerful and versatile enough to support Unix. As of now, in 1998, SCO Unix [38], Linux [32,33,34] and other types of Unix are available on the PC platform. But they are flat and flabby and consume a lot of processor overheads and primary memory. As it is, this type of Unix is not readily suitable for parallel computation. That is, unless the entire kernel is run at each node. That will be tremendously slow and wasteful of hardware resources. What we need is a lean and tight micro-kernel on top of which Unix programs can run at each node. Thus, I developed ways to run programs developed in a Unix environment on the base operating system. I will describe that technique [23] later in this book. That involves putting the processor into a protected mode [24,25] and setting up a flat address space by enabling A20 gating [16]. If today I am asked to make the same decision (namely, about selecting the base operating system) again, I will probably decide differently. I will write a tight micro-kernel that runs in protected mode at each node. The micro-kernel will support the concurrent execution of MS-DOS tasks through a VM86 mode mechanism [24,25,26] and Unix tasks through a native 32-bit mode [24,25] of execution. I do not know enough about Windows, Windows-95 and OS/2 to consider them as prospective base operating systems for the parallel computer.

3.5 Programming language

I decided to support imperative high-level languages. FORTRAN, C and Pascal were the three imperative programming languages for which I implemented runtime libraries for parallel computation. I also implemented the same for one logic programming language (namely, Prolog). I will describe the implementations [27] in this book. One thing that I ensured is that application programs remain portable between our parallel computer and other parallel computers. I also made sure that when the size (in the number of nodes present) of our parallel computer changes, the applications do not have to be rewritten. After some thought, experiments and reading up of literature I developed a technique called *Dimension-independent Parallel Programming* [27,28] that not only ensures that programs are easily portable between our and other parallel computers, but also that the programs do not even have to be recompiled, let alone rewritten, when the size of our own parallel computer changes. I will describe it in this book.

3.6 Guidelines for design

The parallel computer can be a shared memory or a message-passing parallel computer. For a shared memory parallel computer, application programming will be easier. However, it is more difficult to build a practical shared memory parallel computer. The reasons are explained in the next section.

3.6.1 Shared memory

For a shared memory, we have to make the memory address of the shared memory module begin after 640 KB. That region must begin at the hexadecimal address 0A000H:0H. Otherwise, either of the following problems may arise:

- MS-DOS and the applications that are sequential in nature will try to work from the shared memory, thus severely overloading it and degrading performance. The memory access and cycle times too will be non-uniform, making it difficult to write programs with a predictable performance.

- Large sequential applications will not run as they will map into areas of memory that are reserved by the shared memory architecture.

The following problems will arise, on the other hand, if we make the shared memory region begin beyond 640 KB:

- Existing compilers will never generate target codes that place memory objects of interest to the parallel programmer on to the shared memory module. That is because conventional compilers are not designed to work with memory beyond 640 KB. They cannot generate any code which will not run on a conventional IBM PC. If they map codes or data objects onto areas of memory beyond 640 KB, the target program will be incompatible with the conventional IBM PC architecture.

- The holes in the address spaces of the IBM PC beyond 640 KB are not large enough. See Fig. 3.1 for the holes which get created when you use a colour graphics adaptor for your PC. Thus, even if we write our own compiler for the shared memory machine, it will not be possible to accommodate large shared data objects that a parallel programmer might like to keep in a contiguous and shared virtual address space.

- If we make the hole larger, then many memory mapped devices cannot be supported.

And any shared memory machine suffers from the following drawbacks:

- The shared memory cannot be both large and fast.

- Too many processors cannot share the memory at the same time.

- What one processor writes may not be immediately read by another processor and it will be difficult to prevent the reader processor from reading before the writer processor has finished writing.

30   A Practical Approach to Parallel Computing

Additional synchronization hardware has to be built. These mechanisms of sharing and synchronization will not work for a large number of processors.

Therefore, let us drop the idea of building a shared memory parallel computer. For the sake of record, let me mention that I had in fact tried for quite some time, unsuccessfully however, to build a shared memory parallel computer. Nothing much came out of these efforts and I decided to build a message-passing parallel computer which is described in the subsection that follows.

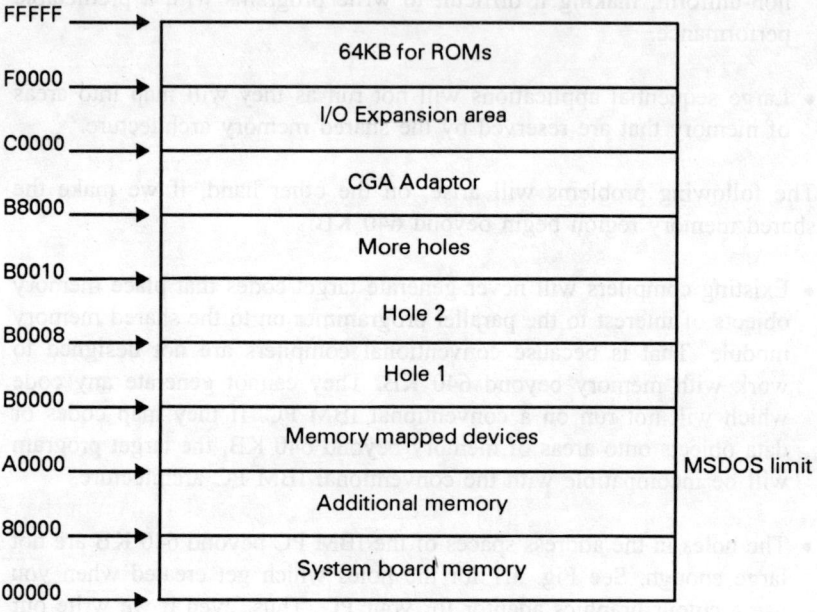

Fig. 3.1   *Memory map of the IBM PC with a CGA adaptor*

3.6.2   Message-passing parallel computers

The width of the holes is sufficient to map message-passing communication hardware. We mapped the hardware on one of the several available holes in the memory map. Typically, we use the first few bytes of the monochrome display adaptor video-RAM addresses to map the interprocessor-communication hardware. On most PCs this works fine, as monochrome adaptors are rarely used. If these addresses have already been taken over by the previously existing hardware like EGA, VGA or SVGA adaptors, we move our links to other holes by changing a PAL [29] equation, as we shall describe later in this book.

The decision to use memory-mapped interprocessor-communication hardware was a bad one. Due to this feature, we cannot have DMA support for our card, as DMA co-processors cannot be programmed to transfer many bytes of data from/to one fixed memory location to/from a range of memory addresses occupied by a region. On the other hand, DMA controllers can be programmed to transfer a block of bytes from/to a byte-wide location in the I/O-address space to/from a region of memory [11]. They indeed work in that mode, for example when handling swap devices [31,32,33,34] in the Unix operating system [30].

At that time, I was not aware of the potential role that DMA can play in making the interprocessor communication

- take place at a high speed,
- independent of the CPU, and
- asynchronous.

in a message-passing parallel computer. Later on, when I understood the relevant issues, I helped someone else [35] develop a better interprocessor-communication interface card. But by that time I had already designed and implemented all the software around the memory-mapped card and invested enough time and effort in that project. It was too late by then to change over to the I/O mapped card. Thus, the memory-mapped card was used to host all the system and application software that I had written about earlier [27,28,36,37] and will describe in this book.

We had also decided on certain other features of our design on the basis of several practical considerations. They are described in the subsections that follow.

Type of link

We decided to design a point-to-point communication link. Routing would be done by the nodes themselves. This makes the link design simple. The CPUs will, however, have to do more work while routing messages. Later on, after we had developed schemes for incorporating routing and buffering of messages as part of the implementation of the runtime environment of our parallel computing paradigm, we developed hardware to automatically route messages. That makes sure nothing is designed which we do not know how to implement, or worse how to use. Throughout this project, I deployed only the minimum amount of specially designed hardware. This strategy paid off well.

Width of link

We decided to have byte-wide communication links. Having serial links will involve developing additional hardware modules to convert bytes into serial bit-streams, only to reassemble them into bytes at the other end.

As the geographical distance is not too much, we might as well transfer bytes between nodes.

Storage at each link

We realized early [39] that storage at each link must be provided to increase the degree of asynchronism between the threads of execution at two nodes connected by a link. The CSP of Charles Anthony Hoare [40] is the most appropriate to serve as a model of parallel computation, for the type of message-passing parallel computer we have decided to build, except that the requirement that the writer process has to wait for the reader would make the throughput of the system rather low. Thus, we wanted to have a mechanism by which the writer can buffer its data under a fixed queueing discipline and proceed, while the reader takes its own time to come to the point in its thread of control where it reads the data. I had tried this earlier with one-byte-long message buffers by implementing them with Intel's 8255 Programmable Peripheral Interface chips [11]. The failure of that approach led me to using as much as possible of the memory I can have at each link. I was fortunate enough to come across the IDT 7203 FIFO chip [41] that has a 2 KB memory, a built-in arbitration logic to enforce a queueing discipline and extra on-chip logic to handle overlapping read and write requests when the FIFO is empty. Figure 3.2 shows the internal block diagram of this chip. I simply designed a lean and thin link between the two PCs built around this chip and never had to look back since then. I had first built a simple interface card that had just one link per card [36]. Later, I built a card that has three links per card, an EPROM to hold the firmware needed for parallel computation, status ports for the links and other advanced hardware features. Most of the software has been written for this card [27]. The largest sized parallel computer that I have assembled until now is a sixteen-processor parallel computer, whose nodes are interconnected in a hypercube, using these cards. Therefore, I will describe the design and implementation of this card in the next chapter.

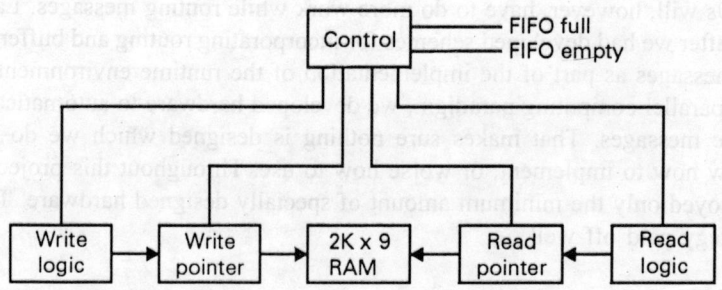

Fig. 3.2   *IDT7203 FIFO chip*

3.7 Exercises

3.7.1 Unix on PCs

1. Can Unix be implemented on an 8088-based PC? If so, why? If not, why not?
2. Name a few unix ports on the IBM PC platform.
3. What is the length of the boot sector on your PC?
4. How do you set up a unix partition on your PC?

3.7.2 BIOS

1. Where does the BIOS EPROM begin in your PC?
2. What is the size of the BIOS EPROM in your PC?
3. How do you make out if the BIOS ROM(s) on your PC motherboard are interleaved?
4. Write a C-callable assembly language program to return the checksum of the BIOS EPROM in your PC.
5. How do you make out if the checksum of your BIOS EPROM is valid?
6. What does POST do, if the BIOS EPROM checksum is invalid?
7. What is the danger in working with a partially corrupted BIOS?
8. What is the possible mechanism for the BIOS EPROM to get corrupted?

3.7.3 Memory map

1. Draw the memory map of your PC.
2. Write an assembly language program to test an area of regular memory on your PC.
3. Does your PC motherboard support extended RAM?
4. Explain how you arrived at the answer to the last question.
5. What is A20 gating?
6. When is A20 gating enabled?
7. When is A20 gating disabled?
8. Write an assembly language program that takes the 80386 CPU to the protected mode and tests for the proper working of extended memory in the address range 4MB to 8MB.
9. Enumerate the properties that a code body must have so that it is rommable, *i.e.* it can be put inside an EPROM and it executes correctly from the EPROM.
10. Draw the memory maps of all the shared memory multiprocessors that you know of.

4
The FIFO Card

Chapter summary

We show the block diagrams of the FIFO card in section 4.1. We explain the organization of the card in detail in section 4.2 and explain how it implements full-duplex communication in section 4.3. How the reader can achieve a better design than the author is explained in section 4.4. Exercises in section 4.5 will further train the reader.

4.1 Block diagrams of the communication card

Each card has three bi-directional full-duplex FIFO links. The block diagram of such a card is shown in Fig. 4.1. One such link between two computers is shown in Fig. 4.2. Each link has a storage capacity of 2 KB. It is built around the IDT 7203 FIFO chip [41] whose block diagram appeared in Fig. 3.2.

4.2 Details of communication card hardware organization

Each card (see Fig. 4.1) can be subdivided into the following blocks:

- **Communication link with FIFO storage**   There are three such links on each card. The FIFO chip is written into by the host PC. The neighbor

The FIFO Card 35

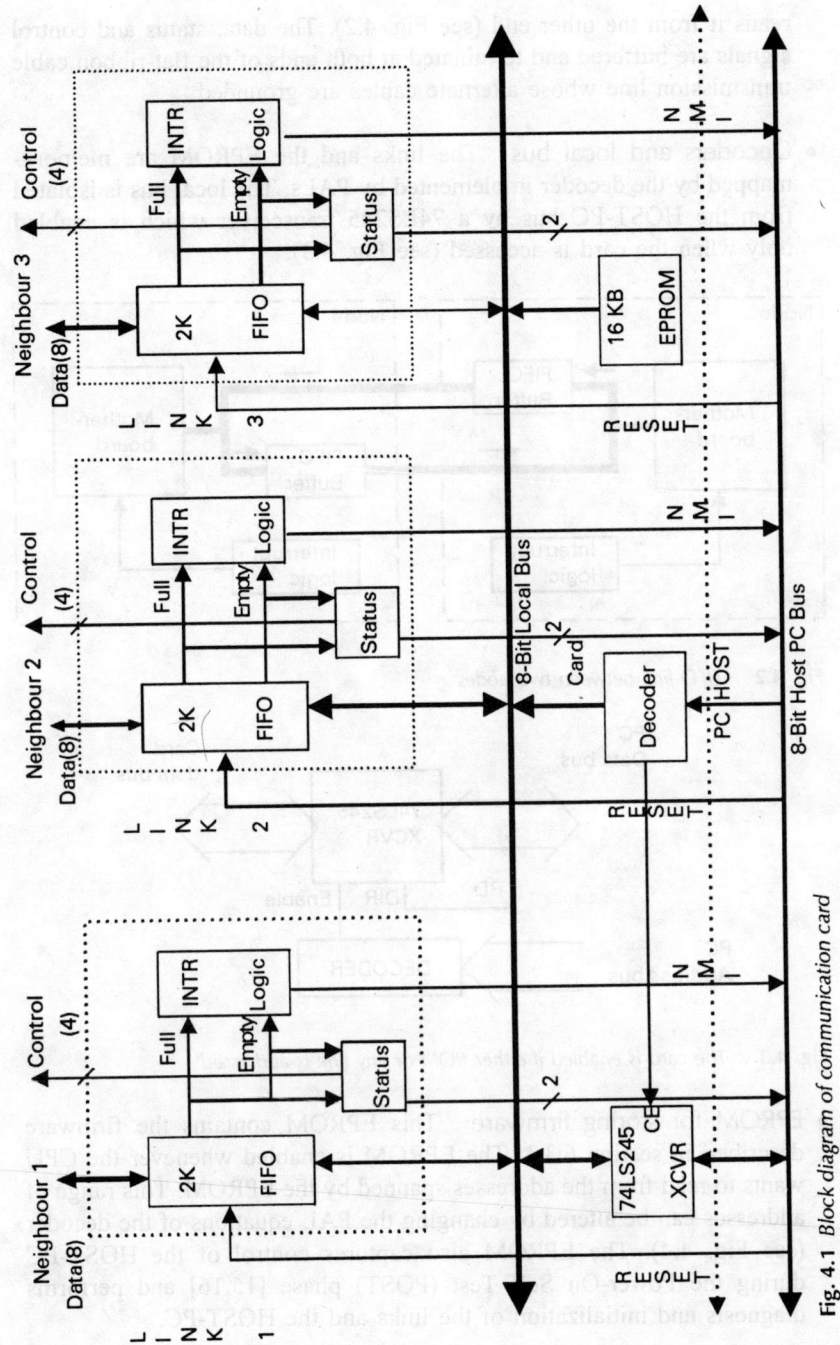

Fig. 4.1 *Block diagram of communication card*

reads it from the other end (see Fig. 4.2). The data, status and control signals are buffered and terminated at both ends of the flat-ribbon cable transmission line whose alternate cables are grounded.

- **Decoders and local bus** The links and the EPROM are memory-mapped by the decoder implemented by PALs. The local bus is isolated from the HOST-PC bus by a 74LS245 transceiver which is enabled only when the card is accessed (see Fig. 4.3).

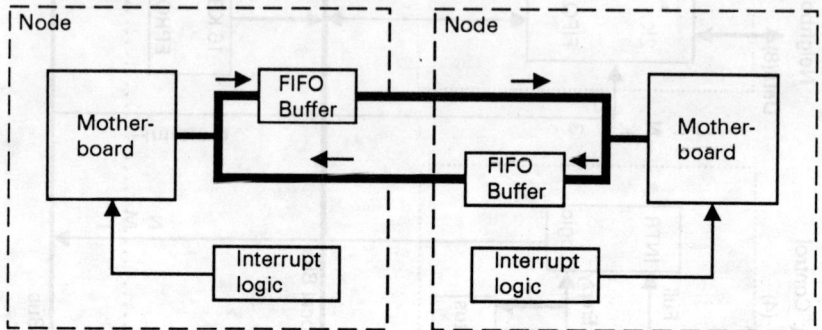

Fig. 4.2   *FIFO link between two nodes*

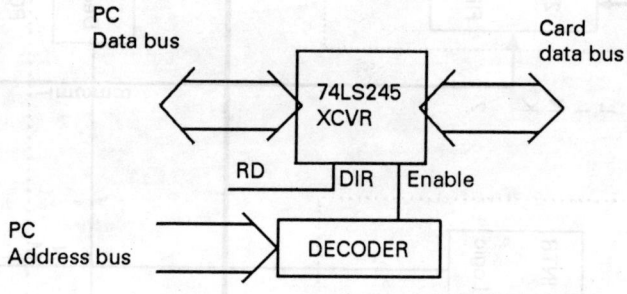

Fig. 4.3   *The card is enabled if either ROM or any link is addressed*

- **EPROM for storing firmware** This EPROM contains the firmware described in section 6.3.1. The EPROM is enabled whenever the CPU wants to read from the addresses spanned by the EPROM. This range of addresses can be altered by changing the PAL equations of the decoder (see Fig. 4.4). The EPROM also captures control of the HOST-PC during the Power-On Self Test (POST) phase [15,16] and performs diagnosis and initialization of the links and the HOST-PC.

- **Interrupt generation logic** Attempts to read from an empty link or write into a full link generates an NMI (Non-Maskable Interrupt) [6,15,16]. This causes the defaulting instruction to be re-tried. Details about this are given in [36].

The FIFO Card   37

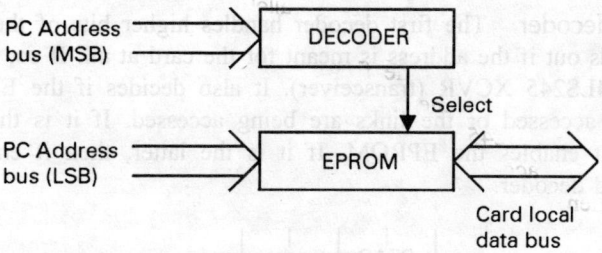

Fig. 4.4   *The ROM is enabled if its range of address is decoded*

- **Status ports and LEDs**   The status of all the links can be read by the HOST-PC from a memory-mapped port. They are also displayed by a number of LEDs on the card.

4.3   Architectural features of FIFO card

The notable hardware architectural features of the add-on FIFO card are:

1. It has memory-to-memory interprocessor communication. Each processor can write into its local FIFO chip and read from its remote FIFO chip in the link. The remote FIFO of one processor is actually the local FIFO of the processor connected to it. (see Fig. 4.2) The data, status and control signals are buffered and terminated at both ends of the flat-ribbon cable transmission line whose alternate cables are grounded. The data lines are buffered at both ends by 74LS245 transceivers whose directions are permanently hard-wired. The outgoing status and control lines are buffered by 7438 open collector NAND-gates. They are terminated at the other end by 390 ohm load resistors.

2. The mechanism of interprocessor message-passing, which we are now describing, incorporates full duplex communication links. This is illustrated in Fig. 4.2. When two processors are interconnected, then processor 1 can write into its own local FIFO and, at the same time, processor 2 can write into processor 2's local FIFO. Thus, there is a two-way communication link between the processors. The two directions of communication are independent of each other.

3. The links support a first-in first-out discipline. That is ensured by the chip [41].

4. The links of the card and the EPROM are memory-mapped by the decoder implemented by PALs. Two commonly available 16L8 PALs [29] are used to produce all the decoding signals as shown in Fig. 4.5.

First decoder The first decoder handles higher bits of the address. It finds out if the address is meant for the card at all. If so, it enables the 74LS245 XCVR (transceiver). It also decides if the EPROM is being accessed or the links are being accessed. If it is the former, then it enables the EPROM. If it is the latter, then it enables the second decoder.

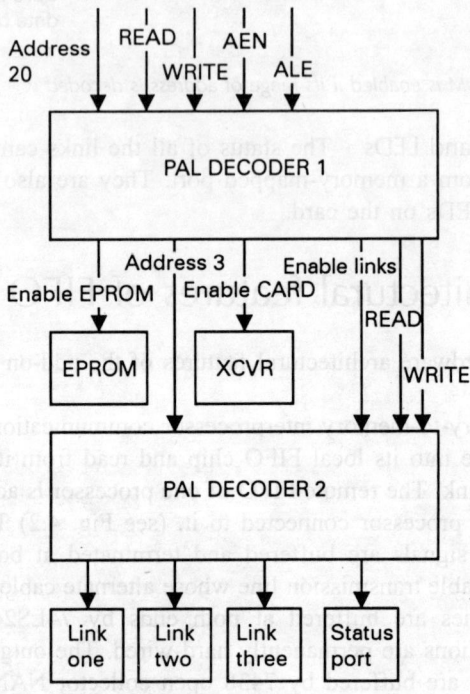

Fig. 4.5 *Two PALs are used to decode*

Second decoder The second decoder distinguishes between the three links and the status port. It produces the read and write signals to the FIFO chips and enables the 74LS374 latch that is used to hold the status of the links.

The addresses and access types of important modules of the FIFO card are described in Table 4.1. The addresses can be easily changed (to make room for memory-mapped devices, if any, that are already mapped onto these addresses) by changing the PAL equations and reprogramming the PALs.

5. If more than three links are required to emanate from a node, more than one card needs to be plugged into the PC. Each additional card provides three more links. Each additional card occupies eight additional byte

locations in the memory address space of the PC. To arrive at the link addresses of the new card, simply add eight to the corresponding address on the old card given in Table 4.1. The additional card(s) cannot have any EPROM. Their EPROMs are disabled by connecting a jumper. If the jumper is on any card, then that card's transceiver does not get enabled even if the valid EPROM address appears on the address bus of the PC.

6. If the link address and/or the EPROM address are modified, then the firmware in the EPROM must be changed to correspond to the new addresses. That is easily done by changing certain 'equate' [13] statements in the assembly language source code of the firmware, assembling and linking the code and writing it into a blank EPROM using an EPROM programmer.

7. The 3 links, the EPROM and the status port have their data lines connected to the local data bus of the card. The local bus is isolated from the host PC by a 74LS245 transceiver, which is enabled only when the card is accessed. The communication card has to be activated for accessing any of the links, accessing the status port, or for accessing the EPROM. All the internal ports and links in this card are memory-mapped. Hence, these have a particular memory address by which they are activated. The direction of data flow between the card and the PC host through the 74LS245 transceiver depends on the current operation in progress on the card. When no operation takes place, the data bus remains tri-stated. The transceiver is then disabled. Table 4.1 summarizes all the types of possible operations.

8. Status polling is supported using memory-mapped ports. The status of all the links can be read by the host PC from the memory-mapped port as a byte. Refer Fig. 4.6 to see how this byte is to be interpreted. They are also displayed by a number of LEDs on the card. Red LEDs indicate FIFO FULL (FF) and green LEDs indicate FIFO EMPTY (FE).

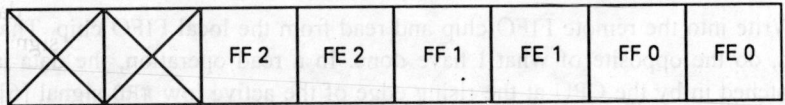

Fig. 4.6 *Interpretation of the status port*

9. Within each card, multicasting [3] is supported. One can write into more than one link simultaneously, if required. This saves a considerable amount of CPU time. For supporting certain types of operations on certain topologies, multicasting is very useful. Thus, we support it in

hardware as can be seen from Table 4.1. Reading simultaneously from more than one link makes no sense. Any link address that attempts to do that does not generate any output from the second decoder. In fact, by suitably reprogramming the two PALs, one can assign special meanings to reads made from such addresses, as in diagnostics for example. In particular, one such address (namely 0xB0000) is used to map the status port, as can be seen from Table 4.1.

Table 4.1 *Addresses of important modules on the FIFO card*

Device Name	Access Type	Begin Address	End Address
EPROM	Read Only	0xD0000	0xD3FFF
Status Port	Read Only	0xB0000	0xB0000
Link One	Read/Write	0xB0006	0xB0006
Link Two	Read/Write	0xB0005	0xB0005
Link Three	Read/Write	0xB0003	0xB0003
All the Three Links Together	Write Only	0xB0000	0xB0000
Links One and Two	Write Only	0xB0004	0xB0004
Links One and Three	Write Only	0xB0002	0xB0002
Links Two and Three	Write Only	0xB0001	0xB0001

4.4 How to improve on this design

If you are designing such a card today, you can avoid some of the mistakes that I made. Also, you can take advantage of the new technologies that have emerged since I froze the design of this card.

4.4.1 Mistakes that you should avoid

Write into remote FIFO

Write into the remote FIFO chip and read from the local FIFO chip. That is, do the opposite of what I have done. In a read operation, the data is latched in by the CPU at the rising edge of the active low #RD signal [6]. Thus, valid data must be presented by the FIFO chip by the time #RD goes high. In order to supply data, the FIFO chip must be enabled. And that enable signal comes from the other end of the link in our design. Thus, the round-trip delay between the two nodes must be less than the read-cycle time of the CPU. Therefore, when there is a large propagation delay between the two nodes, due to a large geographical length between them, the link fails to function, unless wait-states are introduced. Introducing wait-states slows down the rate of data transfer. As of now, the link can have a maximum length of 10 meters for which it can operate with zero wait-states at 40 MHz CPU clock-speed. A better design will rather have the write operations done on remote FIFOs and read operations from local FIFOs. In the case of the write operation, the enable signal and the data to be written can safely race against each other. We are not bothered from this end. We do not need any acknowledgement anyway that the write operation has been successfully completed.

Use horizontal connectors

Use connectors that are parallel to the PCB of the card. That will reduce their height and make them more easily pluggable/unpluggabe. The present design has 40-pin FRC-connectors that are vertical to the PCB. If the personal computer motherboard is already populated with a lot of other cards, it is difficult to remove/insert FIFO cards.

Use I/O mapped links and status port

The idea of interprocessor communication that has been presented so far in this book, as well as the system and application software which we are going to discuss in the subsequent chapters, will work equally well if the FIFO links and the status ports are mapped into the I/O-address space of the PC. In addition, one will be able to use DMA channels to transfer data along the FIFO links. As such, the design which has been presented in this chapter has memory-mapped ports. Thus, DMA cannot be used. That is because no commercially available DMA chip that is used on the IBM PC motherboard can be programmed to transfer data from a block of memory to a single-byte location in the memory address space or vice-versa. On the other hand, all DMA chips can be programmed to transfer data from a block of memory to a single-byte address in the I/O-address space of the PC. That is how they handle block-devices. So, if we had used I/O-mapped ports in our design of the FIFO cards, we could have supported DMA operations along with all else that we support. The use of DMA makes the communication independent of computation, enhances the throughput of the motherboard and makes better use of the storage capacity of the FIFO chips by making block transfers.

4.4.2 New technologies you should use

Since I designed the card, a lot of interesting developments have taken place in the area of hardware design and system integration. I think you can use some of the new technologies that have emerged.

Use EPLDs and FPGAs

Higher density PALs are now available which will make the decoder and other logic fit into one PAL. In fact, you should use EPLDs instead of PALs. FPGAs [42], too, will be useful for implementing a variety of message-handling and message-routing algorithms in hardware. If you use SRAM-based FPGAs, such as the ones from Xilinx [48], these FPGAs can be programmed by your operating system to adaptively configure the message-handling and routing according to the requirements of the application program, in order to extract the maximum performance out of a message-passing parallel computer.

Use a wider data-path

As modern PCs have 32-bit microprocessors, it is wiser to have a 16-bit or a 32-bit data-path. That will mean having to place more than one FIFO chip per card, but now there is room for them, as the glue logic implemented by SSI components can be easily absorbed within the EPLDs or FPGAs.

Put more links per card

These days you can put more links per card as multilayered PCBs are being fabricated in India. Also, all the logic can be compressed into one FPGA part easily, leaving a lot of board space to facilitate routing. You can build a richly connected network of nodes or a hypercube of a higher dimension (by plugging in just one card per node) than what is possible with the present design of the FIFO card, which has only three links per card.

4.5 Exercises

4.5.1 Decoder of an EPROM

1. Write the logic equation for the decoder which produces the #CE signal of an EPROM that starts at the location 0xD0000 and is 32 KB in size. Show how this EPROM is to be interfaced with the PC.

2. Write the logic equations for the two decoders which produce the #CE signal of two EPROMs that start at the location 0xD0000 and 0xD00001 respectively and together span 32 KB in size. The two EPROMs are two-way interleaved. Show how these EPROMs are to be interfaced with the PC.

3. In an advanced motherboard architecture, how does one program of a block of read/write memory act as a read-only memory? Consult the literature on the finite state machines that implement the bus-control logic on your PC motherboard and write a short essay on this subject.

4. What is shadow ROM? Where is it used? Why is it needed?

4.5.2 Better link design

1. Write the logic equations of the second level of the decoder which supports four links per card. Assume that the base address of the links is the same as that of the present card and that it has been decoded by the first level of the decoder.

2. Design the same card, where the base address of the link is programmable from the PC. Latch the base address as a 24-bit number in the three I/O ports with addresses 0x2736, 0x2737 and 0x2738, respectively. Design the decoder for these three port addresses and put three 74LS374s there. From the outputs of these latches, feed signals to the address decoders whose logic equations you are to write down. Draw a block diagram of the entire circuit.

3. Write an essay on how EPLDs and FPGAs can be used to improve on the hardware design presented in this chapter.

5
Putting It All Together

Chapter summary

System integration is explained. Message-passing multicomputers are built using PC motherboards. Scalable topologies are realized. Portable system software is developed. Techniques for maturing our architectures into truly open systems are explained.

5.1 Introduction

Now we are in business! We can build a message-passing parallel computer of any size and topology just by plugging in these cards at each of the nodes and interconnecting the links by 40-core FRC cables. Rather than going for an arbitrary and hasty integration methodology, let us build the parallel computer step by step in a methodical way. That will take us a long way in making our system a truly open system. It will be endowed with the three most important properties of an open system which are:

1. Portability,

2. scalability and

3. interoperability.

We will describe in this chapter how the hardware and system software are integrated.

5.2 Hardware

We describe the board-level organization of each node card and the topology used to interconnect them.

5.2.1 Node-level architecture

Each node has an Intel iSBC386ATZ motherboard, with a 80386 processor, a 80387 co-processor, and 2MB on-board RAM. It works on a 16MHz clock. The boards can be easily upgraded to more powerful and recently designed motherboards, as we have verified by practical experiments, without changing the system or application software in any way.

5.2.2 Topology

We built a four-dimensional hypercube because we had 16 motherboards with us and hypercubes have nice mathematical properties as described in section 1.5.

5.3 Hierarchical design of system software

Rather than driving the FIFO cards directly from the applications, we build the system software in several levels of hierarchy. (see Fig. 5.1) This

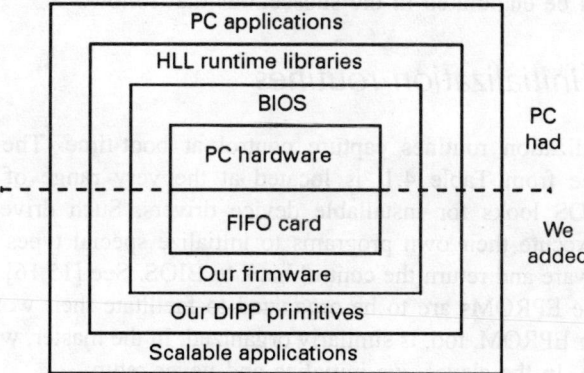

Fig. 5.1 *We match the PC at every level*

has both advantages and disadvantages. The advantages are that we have an open system and things are easy to explain and document. The disadvantages are slow speed of operation and under-utilization of the capabilities of the hardware. There is a similar phenomenon in the erstwhile PC architecture which we have upgraded. That phenomenon I have explained elsewhere [44] Notice also, in our present case, that because we adopted a hierarchical approach (see Fig. 5.1) in designing the system software, we have an open parallel computer architecture which can be used for teaching and research, but some of the capabilities of the hardware (e.g. multicasting) cannot be exploited by all scalable parallel programs that run on this architecture.

In the rest of this chapter, we shall describe all the levels of system software integration of our parallel computer.

5.4 SERC multicomputing firmware

The lower-most level of system software is the SERC multicomputing firmware, described in detail in section 6.3.1. It is the equivalent of BIOS so far as the FIFO card is concerned. Much as BIOS stays physically on the PC motherboard, SERC firmware stays on the FIFO card in an EPROM as described in section 3.6.2 and section 4.2.

Similar to BIOS routines [15,16], the SERC firmware can be logically partitioned into two classes:

1. The initialization routines and

2. the device-driver routines.

These will be elaborated in the subsections that follow.

5.4.1 Initialization routines

The initialization routines capture control at boot-time. The EPROM, as you see from Table 4.1, is located at the very range of addresses where BIOS looks for installable device drivers. Such drivers capture control, execute their own programs to initialize special types of installable hardware and return the control back to BIOS. See [15,16] for details of how the EPROMs are to be organized to facilitate their working with BIOS. Our EPROM, too, is similarly organized. In the master, we initialize and return. In the slaves, we initialize and never return.

Master and slaves

A processor with label zero is called the master. All other processors are organized as slaves. The hypercube is a symmetric architecture. Thus, at runtime, any node can be given the label 0 and with respect to that all other nodes can be dynamically relabelled. All the high-level system software has been implemented taking advantage of this fact. However, during initialization, some identities must be hard-coded. They include the absolute values of the nodeid of each node, dimension of the hypercube, etc. This information is stored in the EPROMs at each node. When the parallel computer is switched off, this information is retained. This information cannot be overwritten by writing an application program and executing it. Thus, this is the ideal way of storing information needed to bootstrap a parallel computer. Once the parallel computer has been bootstrapped using the stored information, application programs can re-label nodes and use a logical dimension that may be different from the physical dimension of the hypercube. Therefore, in the context of initializations, whenever we say 'master', we mean that node whose label is hard-coded to zero. By 'slave', we mean all the other nodes.

Initialization involves:

1. Flushing the FIFO links,

2. carrying out certain repairs on the modules which have become non-functional,

3. setting the board-level system configuration to correct values at each node.

4. correcting the checksum of the CMOS configuration RAM and

5. re-invoking POST.

All these will be discussed in the sections that follow.

The real challenge

If you have read this book so far, you will be able to build a parallel computer. However, bear in mind that details matter. You can build a sixteen-processor parallel computer only after you have the capability to keep all sixteen sequential PCs running properly. And, in India, that is not easy. Look at any laboratory where a number of PCs are installed. You will not find any laboratory where all the PCs work properly. Some of the PCs are only partially functional because of a hardware problem and/or improper initialization. That is because the quality of the components that are dumped into the Indian market by the first-world countries is far worse than what is allowed to be marketed in their own countries. Components which are rejected by their quality control procedures are sent to India. Often, due to complex procurement procedures and other reasons which I better not elaborate here, the end-user does not get to test the quality of components installed in his computer system. So he has to live with the problems. Similarly, frequent power-cuts, low voltages and surges on the power supply lines damage hardware and destroy configuration information. When the system is booted thereafter, manual intervention is needed to restore the configuration and reboot the machine. That is acceptable to the user/administrator of a sequential computer. But for a parallel computer, this must be done automatically and in parallel at all the nodes where damage has been caused to any component and/or the configuration has been destroyed. Otherwise, there is no question of being able to use a parallel computer effectively. Much like a giraffe getting a sore throat, some problems that can be lived with in sequential computation or outside India cannot be ignored when building a parallel computer in India. That is why the SERC firmware performs the last four steps in section 5.3.1, even though *per se* they are not directly related to parallel computation.

Flushing

FIFOs are flushed by reading from the links until they go empty. How many links to flush, is known from the topological constants hard-coded into the EPROMs at each node.

Repair

Certain chips like the real-time clock stop working due to surges. They are restarted by writing certain bit-patterns into certain device registers that are mapped onto the I/O-address space. The diagnostics status byte [16] is examined to see if more on-board components are damaged. If they are, they are repaired by strobing certain bit-fields that are known to repair them. You have to suffer a lot from power supply surges and bad equipment in order to be an expert in all these. In sheer desperation, you learn how to do repairs by writing firmware. And after days and nights of trial and error, you get the bit-patterns and addresses right. I hope you will not have to do what I had to. But if you have to, then only you can help yourself.

Setting the configuration

You know the node-level configuration (like the amount of main memory, number and type of disks, etc.) at each node. Make the firmware write that back into the CMOS configuration RAM, if the old values are destroyed.

CMOS checksum

After you alter any CMOS register value, you must recompute the Modulo-

2^{16} checksum and rewrite it in the designated place in the CMOS RAM. Just remember to skip the first 16 bytes of the RAM, as some of these bytes contain information that change with the passage of wall-clock time.

Re-invoking POST

POST [15,16] is re-invoked by setting the warm-boot flag in the BPB-area to zero. Thereafter, by writing into a device-register within the keyboard-controller chip, the pressing of CTRL-ALT-DEL can be emulated in the firmware. On reboot, POST will think it is a cold boot and thus will redo the diagnostics and set the diagnostic status bytes to the proper values.

5.4.2 Driver routines

They do the low-level device driving in order to implement the primitives of parallel computation elaborated in section 6.3.1.

5.4.3 Who uses the driver routines?

They can be used by any high-level language application program directly [27]. Also, they can be called by the routines which, in turn, implement sophisticated programming paradigms, called *Dimension-independent Parallel Programming (DIPP)*, as given in section 5.4. For more details, see [28].

5.4.4 When does one have to change SERC firmware?

The SERC firmware will change every time the address of the link, the technology used and the physical values of the topological parameters change. That makes sense as the SERC firmware is closely tied to the FIFO link, much as BIOS is to the PC motherboard. And much like the motherboard carries the BIOS ROM, the FIFO card carries the EPROM that has the SERC firmware. Therefore, changing the hardware naturally implies changing the lowermost level of system software in both cases. (see Fig. 5.1)

5.4.5 What the SERC firmware cannot do?

Much like BIOS cannot and does not involve itself with the design philosophy of high-level operating systems, SERC firmware does not bother with or depend on the mathematical properties of topologies or any other high-level issue in distributed operating systems.

5.5 High-level library for scalable distributed computing

This library implements the paradigm called *Dimension-independent Parallel Programming (DIPP)* proposed by me. This library is available in C, FORTRAN, Pascal and Prolog. In this book, only the C-library is explained in detail in section 6.3.2. For the other language routines, see [27] and [28]. Applications can be developed either in an MS-DOS environment or in a Unix environment using the same library of C-callable routines. In the case of the programs developed in a Unix environment, the MUSIX micro-kernel developed by me is used to run the programs on the physical multiprocessor. Details are given in [23] and [45].

5.5.1 Design considerations of the library

Anyone who has designed a parallel algorithm would like to be able to do the following on a given hardware platform, on which he is to implement it:

- Create processes on as many processors as possible
- Terminate them after work is done
- Find out the identity of each process
- Send a message to another process
- Receive a message from another process
- Examine the state of a process at any time

And he would like to express these operations in the language familiar to him.

5.5.2 Specifications of the library

The programming paradigm that the library implements should support sequential computing. On parallel computers, it should support the SPMD style [3] of scheduling with static task-partitioning of data. The executable binary file of the application program should be portable from a sequential computer to an arbitrarily large multiprocessor, with the program finding out at runtime how many processors there are in the multiprocessor, and using all of them.

5.5.3 An epilogue to the library

This library provides a mechanism of doing parallel computation on distributed memory parallel computers. It does not attempt to lay out a policy on how parallel computers are to be programmed. The implementation that I describe in section 6.3.2 is just one implementation. My implementation is restricted to hypercubes. There could be better implementations over better topologies. There can even be many improvements over what I designed as *DIPP* primitives. What I needed to write good parallel programs and implement by myself, is what I designed and implemented.

5.6 Exercises

5.6.1 CMOS RAM

CMOS checksum
1. Write a C-callable assembly language program to find out the checksum of the CMOS RAM. Compare this with the stored value of the checksum.

Real-time clock
1. Find out the time by consulting the real-time clock and display it from a C program.

Main memory
1. Find out how much main memory is present on your system from the configuration RAM.

Extended memory
1. Find out how much extended memory is present on your system from the configuration RAM.

Expanded memory
1. Why is it that the size of expanded memory cannot be stored in the CMOS RAM?

6

Programming Aspects

Chapter summary

This chapter deals mostly with the programming aspects of parallel computers. In this section, we have to think as users of parallel computers. Thus, we have to be critical of existing parallel computer architectures, including the one which we have just designed and built over the last two chapters. After an overview of the development process of parallel application programs in section 6.1, we discuss the design of efficient parallel programs in section 6.1.1. Thereafter, in section 6.2, I shall warn you about bad parallel computers and the people who design and build them. In section 6.3, we will have an overview of the low-level (section 6.3.1) and high-level (section 6.3.2) libraries of system software for parallel computation that we have designed and built. Finally, we describe the E^3-routing in section 6.4 to illustrate how we have built the mechanism for doing any operation over the topology.

6.1 Design of a parallel program

The task of designing a parallel program can be divided into the following parts:

1. Breaking up the algorithm into independent subtasks.

2. Assigning each of these subtasks to different processors in order to execute them in parallel.

3. Identifying the intermediate results of the different processors.

4. Broadcasting these intermediate results to the other processors, if required by the program.

5. Determining the schedule of computation and communication between the different processors.

6. Encoding the algorithm into a suitable programming language.

In order to parallelize an algorithm, it is not generally sufficient to simply divide the sequential algorithm into different parts and assign them to different processors. This may not, in general, lead to a very efficient program. The break-up may not be very homogeneous. In that case, the workload would be different for the different processors. In most cases, it is necessary to manipulate the sequential algorithm so as to break it up into different parallel subtasks. In some cases, the sequential algorithm apparently looks as though it has an inherent parallelism, but it may not be very efficient when executed in parallel.

The efficiency of a parallel program also depends on the architecture and node-level performance of the parallel machine. The peak performance and structure of the parallel programs that run optimally on a given architecture, are estimated by quantifying the following:

1. t_{calc} This is the time required to perform any generic calculation, for example a floating point calculation $(a = b + c)$ or $(a = b * c)$.

2. t_{comm} This is the time required to communicate a single word between any two nodes of the parallel machine.

The average performance depends not only on the time taken for a floating point calculation, but also on the location of the storage of these numbers. Thus, the data-structures of an efficient parallel program have to be carefully designed for it to work efficiently on a distributed memory parallel computer architecture. The next subsection explains this in more detail.

6.1.1 Efficient parallel programming techniques

When you write programs to do numerical linear algebra, or for that matter any computation that features multidimensional arrays on distributed memory parallel computers, remember that if at any processor's local memory you change a variable, the copy of the same variable held at all the other processors' local memories are not affected. Thus, you must explicitly update these copies, in order to produce a correct result of the computation. You must send the new value of the variable to all other nodes by invoking some kind of a *send* system call. We discuss the syntax and semantics of this call in our own machine in this chapter (see section 6.3.2). For details about other machines, look up information about the particular parallel computer which you are trying to program.

The syntax and semantics of these calls vary from one parallel computer to another. The only common thing perhaps, that runs across all these computers is the enormous amount of time, called *communication overheads*, spent in sending the values to update the other copies. If you want more parallelism to be exploited in any distributed memory computer, you must have more number of copies of the same variable in the virtual address spaces of different CPUs. The virtual address spaces are disjoint. And having more number of copies only makes the system take longer to update all of them. If it did not, the architecture would be *scalable*. No parallel computer architecture is scalable, though many parallel computer architects claim that their architecture is scalable. So you, the numerical analyst, will probably have to work with one of the existing architectures before a truly scalable architecture is built.

When you work with non-scalable architecture, you will see that it takes hundreds or even thousands of CPU cycles of communication overhead to transfer a word from a local memory to update other copies, whereas in a couple of clock cycles, rather powerful floating point arithmetic and other operations can be performed between operands placed within the local memory. And much of this overhead comes in due to the very many levels of hierarchy within the system software organization of practical parallel computers (see Fig. 5.1). This means that even if you transfer only a few bytes from your local memory, you have to incur an enormous amount of overheads.

The hardware of the communication mechanism is not usually slow across parallel computers. It is just that in order to get to the hardware, you have to make your program invoke so many levels of system software and pass parameters between them. Thus, it is a better idea to invoke *send* only once to transmit 1000 bytes of updated information, rather than make two calls to *send*, each requesting to transmit 500 bytes. So, a smart parallel programmer packs in all the updated variables (whether or not these variables have got any correlation among themselves) in one block of memory which (s)he organizes as an one-dimensional array and thereafter transmits the whole array with one call to *send*. This is called *marshalling* and its proper use, depending on the realities of the parallel computer in question, transforms the subject of writing efficient parallel programs into an art form. And much like any other art form, it is misused as a tool of deception by those who have mastered the art and want to cheat. We will review the philosophy and product of this type of people in the next section, as you will have to live with them if you have to use parallel computers.

6.2 How to make a bad parallel computer...

... and get away with it! Here is how you go about it.

Select the best high-performance CPU of the day from a well-known CPU vendor. Do not try to build a motherboard that is most appropriate for your kind of parallel computer architecture. Buy off-the-stock motherboards from unknown vendors who cannot even supply you with the details of the board-level organization. You will not need them.

Do not try to connect these boards usually supported with fast communication channels needed for a good message-passing architecture. That will be too much trouble to design and build. The motherboard must be supporting some form of networking either by fiber-optic channels or the old-fashioned Ethernet. Use this mechanism and call it your special-purpose channels.

Do not write drivers with low overheads for these channels. Who will debug them during development? Incorporate all the levels of device drivers and their protocols, even if they have nothing to do with supporting parallel computation.

Do not write operating systems. Buy it. Do not even try to adapt it for parallel computation. If you can, get hold of the implementation details of the operating system, but do not read them. Nor should you try to modify the operating system in any way. Just make sure that the networking functions at the highest level are working correctly to some extent, albeit with a huge overhead.

Do not try to write a special-purpose compiler. Just spread the rumour that you are writing one. Instead, write a library of system calls that invokes the networking software to transfer data. Using this library, write a suite of demonstration programs that partition the computational task across two CPUs. Select an application problem that involves very little data-transfer while the program is executing. But keep the computational load deliberately enormous. Good demonstration applications are numerical integration (compute double and triple integrals for better effect – chances are nobody will ever ask you where you will use the end-result), statistical computations and the like. If you are asked about how your computer performs in numerical linear algebra, do careful *marshalling* and show good speedups for two processors. Extrapolate your speedups by ordinary arithmetic to computers using thousands and millions of such CPUs. That will make sure you will not be asked to actually build them. Call your computer a supercomputer.

If you come across another group of computer architects who cheat people the same way, call your computer a special purpose parallel computer. If both of you are called to a common forum, call your own computer the best computer "of its kind".

Deliver, if you have to, one prototype to a user-site and promptly forget all about it thereafter. Some poor numerical analyst there will have to suffer (and his boss will think he cannot write efficient parallel programs after the boss has seen your demos), while you are already talking of your next architecture.

6.3 Routines facilitating parallel programming

The low-level routines are written in assembly language and frozen in EPROMs at each node. They are described in section 6.3.1. These routines are callable from C and any other high-level language that can invoke traps (in Intel and IBM PC parlance, such traps are called *interrupts*) to the operating systems for getting services from the operating system.

The high-level routines are written in C. Section 6.3.2 describes them. These routines are callable from C and other high-level languages for which I have implemented the **Dimension-independent Programming Paradigm (DIPP)**. The high-level routines eventually call the low-level routines in order to drive the FIFO links.

6.3.1 Elementary routines

These routines implement the primitives of parallel computation. More complex routines, described in section 6.3.2 are built on top of them. All these routines have been firmwared and they are invoked by interrupt INT 0x60 with unique subfunction numbers. A brief description of each of these routines is given below:

Function: fork

Purpose: To spawn a thread of computation in the nodes at the other end of the links identified by mask.

Syntax: int fork(int mask) from a C application.

Invocation: Invoked by INT 60H function AH=5.

Implementation: Coded in assembly language and put in EPROMs.

Operation: The following steps are executed by the fork function:
1. It finds the conventional memory size (by executing INT 12H) in KB available in the system.
2. It shifts this quantity by six bits to the left (and filling in with zeroes) locations to convert it into the number of paragraphs.
3. It checks whether the code segment, data segment and the stack segment can be accommodated in the available memory. In case the available memory is less, it exits the fork with a proper error code in the AH register.
4. Fork calls the transfer function to transmit code. The transfer function needs the length of the data to be transferred in CX and the start of code segment address in ES. Transfer first transmits CX and ES to the slave (the slave will be executing the receive function), so that the slave knows how many bytes to receive and where to put those bytes. Then transfer (running on master) and transmit (running on slave) together execute to transmit CX number of bytes starting from ES:00.
5. The same steps are executed for transmitting the data segment.
6. The stack is copied in a different way, as transfer and receive copy only forward and stack has to be copied backwards. For copying stack, the following steps are executed:
   a) First ES is made to point to SS:SP:

$$ES \leftarrow SS + SP/16. \qquad (6.1)$$

   After this ES:0 points to SS:SP
   b) The length of the stack to be copied is obtained from the fork parameters. Then the transfer function is called. By doing so, some extra bytes (less than 16) are also copied.
   Example 6.1 Let SS = 2000H and SP = 0026H. Assign the effective address EA $\leftarrow$ SS * 16 + SP. Thus, EA = 20026H. But, ES = AX/16 = 2002H. So stack transfer takes place from 2002:00 and not from 2002:6. Thus, six extra bytes are transmitted. After the master transfers SS and SP to the slave, the slave will also be pointing to 2000:0026. Thus, ignoring those extra six bytes.
   c) The master then sends the SS and SP values. Thus, the master and the slave will then have exactly same code, data and stack.
7. The master returns to the next instruction after the call to fork in the program. The slave is also made to return to the next instruction in the program.

Function: bread

Purpose: To read a block of bytes from a unique link identified by mask.

58   A Practical Approach to Parallel Computing

Syntax: `void bread(int mask, char far* addr,int size)`

Invocation: Invoked by INT 0x60 function 2.

Implementation: Coded in assembly language and put in EPROM.

Operation: bread reads data of size specified by `size`, from the FIFO link, into the memory location specified by `addr`. The call to bread is blocking, in the sense that unless all the data has been read into the buffer, the control does not return to the caller. The following steps are executed:
1. It checks for the existence of the EPROM.
2. It identifies the FIFO link from the mask.
3. It computes the effective byte pattern with which to compare, in order to determine if the link is empty
4. It calls a subroutine inside the EPROM to perform a blocked read.
5. The subroutine polls the link in a loop. If it is empty, it waits. Or else it reads in a byte from the link and places it in the buffer.

Function: bwrite

Purpose: To write a block of bytes into a set of links identified by mask.

Syntax: `void bwrite(int mask, char far *addr, int size)`

Invocation: Invoked by INT 0x60 function 1.

Implementation: Coded in assembly language and put in EPROM.

Operation: bwrite writes blocked data of size specified by `size`, into the FIFO link, from the memory location specified by `addr`. The following steps are executed in a bwrite implementation:
1. It checks the existence of the EPROM.
2. It calculates the checksum.
3. It identifies the FIFO link from the mask.
4. It calls an internal routine in the EPROM to perform a blocked write on the link identified by mask.

Function: dimhyp

Purpose: To get the dimension of the hypercube

Syntax: `void dimhyp(int *dim)`

Invocation: Invoked by INT 0x60 function 8.

Implementation: The body is coded in assembly language and put in EPROM. The C-callable interface and the portion that checks for valid EPROM is coded in C and linked by the C link-editor.

Operation: dimhyp calculates the dimension of the hypercube and assigns the value to dim, by serially executing the steps stated below:
1. It checks the presence of the EPROM. If there is no EPROM, it sets dimension to zero.
2. Calculates the checksum.
3. Looks up the dimension of the hypercube stored in the EPROM.

Function: nodeid

Purpose: To return the label of the node

Syntax: `int nodeid(void)`

Invocation: Invoked by INT 0x60 function 8.

Implementation: The body is coded in assembly language and put in EPROM. The C-callable interface and the portion that checks for valid EPROM is coded in C and linked by the C link-editor.

Operation: nodeid identifies the binary label associated with the node. It returns the node ID, after performing the following steps:
1. Checks the presence of the EPROM. If there is no EPROM, it returns zero.
2. Calculates the checksum.
3. Looks up a value stored in the EPROM for obtaining the node's identity.

Function: terminate

Purpose: To terminate a thread of computation

Syntax: `void terminate(void)`

Implementation: The body is coded in assembly language and put in

EPROM. The C-callable interface and the portion that checks for valid EPROM is coded in C and linked by the C link-editor.

Invocation: Invoked by INT 0x60 function 6.

Operation: The terminate routine terminates a process. After this is executed, the processor is ready for another process to be spawned on it again. The steps which are implemented by the terminate routine are:
1. It checks the presence of the EPROM. If there is no EPROM, it exits out of the present program and goes back to the operating system.
2. It calculates the EPROM checksum. If EPROM is valid, it goes to the next step.
3. For zero nodeid, it returns control to the base operating system. For non-zero nodeids, it jumps to the beginning of the program within EPROM that awaits a fresh program download from any of its neighbors.

Symmetry among low-level routines

Note that `fork()` and `terminate()` are symmetric routines that must work concurrently. If one is executing at one end of any link, the other must be executing at the other end of the same link.

Similarly, `bread()` and `bwrite()` are symmetric routines. Not only must they execute together and concurrently at both ends of a FIFO link, the number of bytes sought to be transferred must be the same for both the functions.

Failure to maintain these two conditions will result in one or more of the following problems:

Wrong Results will be generated by parallel programs.

Deadlocks will stall the entire multiprocessor.

Slow Speed will make it irritating to use the multiprocessor.

Race Conditions will make results irreproducible on the multiprocessor.

The onus is on the application programmer to make sure that symmetry is maintained among the low-level routines.

SERC firmware's counterpart of POST

After initialization of the FIFO links, on power up or hardware reset,

- the master invokes the bootstrap function INT 19H to load the higher-level operating system, *e.g.* MS-DOS.

- the slaves jump to terminate() directly. From then onwards, they load and run any executable program downloaded via the links.

Note the following:

- Half of the operation of fork() is actually done from the body of the executable code of terminate(), as can be seen from the description of how fork() works.

- Any slave can boot from any link. Within the body of terminate(), the thread of control waits for any link to go non-empty. Thereafter, it downloads all the executable code and the data/stack image from that link, as per the length information which comes along in the header.

6.3.2 Complex routines

More complex routines are implemented by writing programs in C. Their object code is linked with the application program by the C compilation system. These functions honour the parameter-passing convention of the high-level language (*viz.* C in this book), in which the application programs (*i.e.* the caller of these routines) are written. In order to understand how these routines are implemented, the following assumptions have to be made:

Assumption 6.1 Consider a d-dimensional hypercube with $D = 2^d$ nodes. Each node has a local copy of each variable. If a node N_1 is directly connected with another node N_2, then N_1(parent) can spawn a process on N_2 (child). The values of all variables in the parent program are inherited by the child. The child and parent resume execution from that point. Thereafter, any update to any local copy does not affect the other copies at the other nodes. The local copy of a variable var1 at Node N_i is denoted var1@N_i. When the '@' is omitted, it means 'everywhere'. The statements between the **cobegin** and **coend** pairs are executed in parallel, in all the D nodes.

Function: forkall

Syntax: void forkall(void)

Semantics: Initiates a thread of computation at every available node.

Algorithm: It works as follows:

Input: Program executing at Node 0;

Output: Program executing at all the D nodes;

```
procedure forkall;
var  idim, nsrc, ndst :integer;
     active :boolean;
```

Initially: active@0 = true, active@i = false if $i \neq 0$

```
begin
nsrc := 0;
   for  idim:= 0 to d - 1 do
        cobegin
           ndst := nsrc + 2^idim;
           if active then nsrc spawns on ndst;
           active@ndst := true;
           nsrc@ndst := ndst;
        coend
end;
```

Function: termall

Syntax: void termall(void)

Semantics: Terminates execution at each node.

Algorithm: It works as follows:

Input: Program executing at all the D nodes;

Output: All the D nodes ready to execute another parallel program;

```
procedure termall;
begin
     At Node 0, return control back to the command shell.
     Elsewhere, return control to
     the multiprocessing firmware.
end;
```

Function: numpro

Syntax: int numpro(void)

Semantics: Returns the number of processors in the system.

Algorithm: Get the value of the dimension d frozen at each node. Return 2^d to the caller.

Function: scatter

Syntax:
```
void scatint(int *)
void scatflt(float *)
void scatdbl(double *)
void scatany(char *) /* Scatters Anything */
```

Semantics: Copies value of the variable at node 0 to all other processors.

Operation: It works as follows:

Input: var1@0 = val1;

Output: var1@i= val1, $\forall i \in [0 \ldots D-1]$;

Procedure scatter works like forkall, except that instead of spawning task nsrc sends val1 to ndst.

Function: gather

Syntax:
```
void gathint(int *)
void gathflt(float *)
void gathdbl(double *)
```

Semantics: Combines values of the variable at all nodes at processor zero.

Operation: It works as follows:

Input: var1@i = val1$_i$; $\forall i \in [0 \ldots D-1]$;

Output: $\biguplus_{i=0}^{D-1}$ val1$_i$@0, where $\biguplus$ stands for *combination*;

```
procedure gather;
var   idim:integer;
      active:boolean;
      val1, tmp1:anytype;
```

Initially: active@i = true $\forall i \in [0 \ldots D-1]$

```
begin
    for idim:=d-1 downto 0 do
        cobegin
```

```
            if active and  nodeid ≥ 2^{idim} then
                begin
                    Send val1 to neighbor with
                    label = nodeid - 2^{idim};
                    active := false;
                end
            if active and nodeid < 2^{idim} then
                begin
                    Receive tmp1 from neighbor with
                    label = nodeid + 2^{idim};
                    val1 := val1 ⊎ tmp1;
                end
        coend
end;
```

Function: make_Consistent

Syntax: fromany(char far *value, int numbyt, int srcpe)

Semantics: Updates copies of a variable of *any type* occupying numbyt bytes of storage with the value of the same variable to which it is bound at the processor with nodeid=srcpe.

Algorithm: Let '⊕' denote the exclusive-OR operation.

Input: var1[i]@i = val1$_i$, $\forall i \in [0 \ldots D-1]$, var1[j]@i is undefined when $i \neq j$.

Output: var1[i]=val1$_i$, $\forall i \in [0 \ldots D-1]$

```
procedure make_Consistent;
var   idim, iproc:integer;
      active:boolean;
      var1:array [0 ... D - 1] of anytype;
begin
    for iproc := 0 to D - 1 do
        begin
            active@iproc := true;
            src := iproc ⊕ nodeid;
            for  idim :=0 to d - 1 do
                if active then
                cobegin
                    dst := src + 2^{idim};
                    Send var1[iproc]@src;
                    Receive var1[iproc]@dst;
                    active@dst := true;
```

```
            coend;
        active := false;
      end;
end;
```

Different approach

While designing an application program that will use the high-level functions, you tend to look at the entire multiprocessor or a sub-topology thereof. You do not have to take a link-by-link approach as in low-level programming. Thus, your programs are ensured to be correct and deadlock-free. They are more portable to other parallel computers, but you lose in terms of performance and speed slightly. That is because of the overheads in executing the DIPP routines themselves. See Fig. 5.1.

6.4 The E-cube routing scheme

The E-cube routing was originally proposed by Sullivan and Bashkow in 1977. It is a form of deterministic routing, i.e. the communication path is uniquely predetermined by the source and destination addresses, independent of the network conditions.

Consider the binary label of the source node to be $s = s_{n-1}s_{n-2}\ldots s_0$, and that of the destination node to be $d = d_{n-1}d_{n-2}\ldots d_0$, for a n-dimensional hypercube with 2^n nodes. Let $v = v_{n-1}v_{n-2}\ldots v_0$ be the binary label of any node along the route. The following steps are sequentially executed in the routing process:

1. For all n dimensions, the direction bit is calculated, i.e $r_i = s_{i-1} \oplus d_{i-1}$, where r_{i-1} is the ith direction bit, i ranging from 1 to n.

2. Set dimension = 1 and $v = s$.

3. If $r_i = 1$, the current node is routed to the next node. The next node is determined by evaluating $v \oplus 2^{i-1}$.

4. $i = i + 1$

5. If $i < n$, go to step 2.

As an example, consider a four dimensional hypercube topology. Let the binary label of the source node be 1000 and that of the destination be 1111.

The E-cube routing is executed as follows:
Here $s = 1000$ and $d = 1111$.

1. $r_1 = 0 \oplus 1 = 1$, $r_2 = 0 \oplus 1 = 1$, $r_3 = 0 \oplus 1 = 1$ $r_4 = 1 \oplus 1 = 0$.

2. dimension = 4, and $v = 1000$.

3. $r_1 = 1$, thus, $v = 1000 \oplus 0001 = 1001$. $r_2 = 1$, thus, $v = 1001 \oplus 0010 = 1011$. $r_3 = 1$, thus, $v = 1011 \oplus 0100 = 1111$.

Thus, the route is obtained, with the different values of v being the node labels of the intermediate nodes.

6.5 Exercises

6.5.1 Routing messages

1. In a 10-dimensional hypercube, trace the path of an E^3-routed message as it goes from node 433 to node 845. How many hops will the message take?

2. Write a C function void tracerout(unsigned int src, unsigned int dst, int dimhyp) which traces the path of a message from a node with label src to a node with label dst in a hypercube with dimension dimhyp.

3. Describe the routing algorithm in a mesh and compare it with the E^3-routing algorithm of a hypercube.

4. Explain how you can implement the E^3-routing algorithm in hardware using FPGAs in a monograph.

6.5.2 Relabelling hypercubes

1. In a 6-dimensional hypercube, arrive at an original scheme of labelling. Label all the nodes of the hypercube accordingly. Thereafter, refer to the node 34 as node 0. In this new scheme of labelling, put labels on all the nodes.

2. Write a mathematical formula that returns the new label of an old nodeid, for a hypercube of a given dimension where an arbitrary node, say node with label n_1 has been relabelled as node zero.

3. Write a C function unsigned int newlabel(unsigned int oldlabel, unsigned int newzero, int dimhyp) which computes the new label of any node in a relabelled hypercube.

7
Example Applications

Chapter summary

In the last chapter, some of the important routines used for encoding parallel programs were discussed. In this chapter, some important features of programming are highlighted using certain model programs. All the programs are encoded on the basis of the hypercube architecture of the parallel machine.

7.1 Dimension independent programs

Programs which are not dependent on the dimension of the hypercube topology are called dimension independent programs. As already stated in Chapter 1, the number of processors directly connected to a given processor (host PC) in the hypercube topology gives the dimension of the hypercube.

Programs which can run without any change on any multicomputer with the hypercube architecture, irrespective of the dimension of the hypercube are termed as dimension independent programs. These programs also run successfully on sequential computers, as a sequential computer can be considered to have a hypercube architecture of dimension zero.

A simple dimension independent program that was coded, approximates the value of π by numerically evaluating

$$\pi = \int_0^1 \frac{4}{(1+x^2)} = \frac{1}{N} \sum_{j=1}^n \frac{4}{(1+x_j^2)}, \qquad (7.1)$$

where N is the number of intervals the given integral is divided into to enhance parallel computing. Also,

$$x_j = (j - 0.5)/N. \tag{7.2}$$

Virtually all the work is done in a single loop. The inner loop is parallelized on many parallel systems. This program was run by Karp *et al.* [5] on nine commercially available multiprocessors:

1. Alliant FX/8

2. BBN Butterfly

3. Cray X-MP/48

4. ELXSI6400

5. Encore Multimax

6. Flex/32

7. IBM 3090/VF

8. Intel iPSC

9. Sequent Balance 21000

It was also run on the SERC multicomputer which has a hypercube architecture of dimension 4. It was also run on a sequential computer and the speedup was noted down for different values of N.

In the sequential program, the number of intervals is first read in and then its reciprocal is calculated. The sum is at first initialized to zero. The final sum is calculated in a loop which is executed N times, each iteration incrementing the value of the sum by

$$4/(1 + x_j^2). \tag{7.3}$$

The error is calculated by comparing the analytical value and that obtained numerically.

In the parallel machine, each processor calculates, in parallel, the value of the function for a few intervals. Each processor then broadcasts the values it has calculated to the other processors. Finally, the zeroth processor (host PC) gathers the values and sums them up to obtain the desired result. The program is listed in Fig. 7.1. The speedup of the parallel machine for different values of N is tabulated in Table 7.1. For small values of N, the speedup was negligible. This is because forking and the other parallel routines take up a lot of time, thus increasing the total computational time. For less data, these overheads take up most of the computational time, and, thus, the sequential machine is faster. But, for a large amount of data, the computational time increases considerably. The time taken for forking, etc. become negligible in comparison. The speedup thus increases. In the above program, the speedup was found to asymptotically reach 15.

```
forkall(); nid=nodeid(); np=numproc(); psm=0.0;
nd=1.0/((double) intrvl); intrvl=40000;
st_tm=timetick(); for(i=nid+1;i<=intrvl;i+=np)
psm += f(((float)i-0.5)*nd);
psm*=nd; gprd((double far *)&psm); ftm=timetick();
if(!nid)  { api=4.0*atan(1.0);
           printf("\ntime = %d\n",(ftm-st_tm));
}
else
    terminate();
```

Fig. 7.1 A scalable program to compute π

Table 7.1 Speedups for different intervals for computing π

N	S	P	SP
500	0	2	0
1000	0	2	0
5000	4	2	2
9000	8	2	4
10000	9	2	4.5
12500	11	2	5.5
17500	16	2	8
20000	18	3	6
50000	45	5	9
70000	62	6	10.33
100000	89	8	11.125
200000	177	14	12.64
300000	269	20	13.45
400000	355	26	13.65
500000	447	32	13.9
1000000	894	63	14.19
2000000	1787	122	14.64
3000000	2661	182	14.62

7.2 The manybody problem

The manybody problem is an ideal example to measure the efficiency of the parallel computer, as there is intensive communication between the different processors.

If there exists a system of N_p particles that interact via a pair potential, then the total potential energy of the system consisting of such particles is given by

$$U = \frac{1}{2} \sum_{i=1}^{N_p} \sum_{j=1}^{N_p} \phi(\vec{x_i}, \vec{x_j}), \qquad (7.4)$$

where $\phi(\vec{x_i}, \vec{x_j})$ is the pair potential or the potential energy between the ith and the jth particle.

$$\phi(\vec{x_i}, \vec{x_j}) = -\frac{Gm_i m_j}{|\vec{x_i} - \vec{x_j}|}, \qquad (7.5)$$

where G is the gravitational constant, $\vec{x_i}$ is the position vector of the ith particle, whose mass is m_i.

The manybody problem is to compute the potential energy, U, of the system.

The algorithm is as follows:

1. Find the dimension of the hypercube.

2. Calculate the total number of processors working in parallel in the machine.

3. Start all the processors.

4. Find out the identity of each node of the hypercube topology.

5. Assign boundaries to each processor.

6. Initialize the particle data at each processor for its partition.

7. Broadcast each partition to all other processors.

8. Compute the potential energy at each processor.

9. Sum up all the potential energy at processor zero and print the result.

The manybody problem was coded in Turbo C and Turbo Pascal in an MS-DOS environment. It can handle up to 1600 particles. This problem exposes high communication overload in step 7. The speedup of the problem is given in Table 7.2. For a few bodies the speedup was negligible, as the time taken for communication between the links was dominant over the time taken for the calculation of potential energy. For a large number of bodies, the computational time increased considerably, thus increasing the speedup. The speedup was found to asymptotically reach 13. This difference in the asymptotic value of the speedup as compared to the calculation of π, was due to the increase in communication between the processors.

Table 7.2 Speedup for the manybody problem

No. of bodies	Seq. time	speedup
16	0.38	0.034
32	2	0.1818
64	6	0.5
128	22	1.6923
256	90	5.0
320	139	6.95
384	201	8.04
480	314	9.8125
512	358	10.2286
640	558	10.7306
800	874	11.9726
864	1020	12.4878
928	1176	12.6452
1024	1440	12.8571

7.3 The Diophantine predicate satisfiability problem

$\mathcal{N}$ is the set of natural numbers $0, 1, 2, 3 \ldots$, and let S_i, $i = 1, \ldots, k$ be k subsets of $\mathcal{N}$, whose elements are chosen at random.

Let $\hat{S} = S_1 \times S_2 \times \ldots \times S_k$. Let $\hat{S} \supset \tilde{S}$, $\tilde{S} = (q_1, q_2, \ldots, q_k) \in \hat{S} \mid_{PL(q_1, q_2, \ldots, q_k)}$ holds where p_L is a k-ary diophantine predicate. The problem is to find out the cardinality of $\tilde{S}$, i.e $\mid \tilde{S} \mid$.

The implementation of this problem indicates how a CSP-like parallelism can be efficiently supported in a logic programming system. This program was coded in Turbo Prolog, in the MS-DOS environment. The Diophantine predicates are as follows

$$3x_1 + 4x_2 + 5x_3 - 2x_4 = \text{RHS}, \tag{7.6}$$

$$2x_1 - 3x_2 + 4x_3 - 6x_4 < 500, \tag{7.7}$$

$$x_1 + 2x_2 - 3x_3 - 3x_4 > 50, \tag{7.8}$$

$$-4x_1 + 5x_2^2 - x_3 + 5x_4 > 100, \tag{7.9}$$

where $x_1 \in [1, 256]$, $x_2 \in [1, 16]$, $x_3 \in [1, 32]$, $x_4 \in [1, 32]$.

This program was solved by exhaustive enumeration of Prolog's built-in inference engine. The first set of x_1 was partitioned into 16 disjoint subsets in the parallel program. The speedup was found to be 15.4 as against the ideal case of 16, and was independent of the RHS.

7.4 The 2-D image recognition problem

The input was the two images A_1 and A_2. The output was the rotation θ, translation $\vec{x}$ and scaling s done to A_1 so that the two images match. The main aim was to reduce the problem to an optimization problem. The algorithm is as follows:

1. Image A_1 was rotated by an angle θ, translated by $\hat{x}$ and scaled by a factor s to get an image $\bar{A}_1$.

2. The number of mismatches between A_2 and $\bar{A}_1$ was noted down.

3. The number of mismatches was a function of $\theta, \vec{x}$ and s. The function was represented as $f(\theta, \vec{x}, s)$.

4. Minimize $f(\theta, \vec{x}, s)$.

The problem was coded in Turbo C and Turbo Pascal. The pixel matrix was partitioned by rows in a dimension independent parallel program. The maximum number of pixels used was 160×160 and the speedup at that size was found to be 15.1.

7.5 Exercises

7.5.1 Developing application programs

1. Initialize a floating point variable to 1.0 at node 0. Write a dimension-independent program to scatter that value to all the nodes in the multicomputer, increment them by 9.0 in parallel at each node and gather their sum at node 0.

7.5.2 Developing system programs

1. Write a C function that gathers strings (null-terminated strings, as C strings are) at every node of a multicomputer and returns a concatenation of all the strings at processor zero. The program must be scalable.

2. Formulate how you will implement the following multicomputing-specific operations in a scalable fashion, on a torus:

   - `forkall()`
   - `scatter()`
   - `gather()`
   - `make_Consistent()`

3. Encode the above algorithms in C. Assume the same low-level routines, which were explained in Chapter 6 of this book to be present, implemented in EPROMs at every node of the torus and the torus being put together using FIFO links as explained in the Chapter 5.

4. Write the `gather()` function for single-precision reals that return a NaN, if any of the values at the nodes from where the sum is gathered has a quiet NaN in place of the floating point variable.

8

Case Studies

Chapter summary

In the last chapter, four parallel programs were cited. The calculation of π was given as an example of a dimension independent program, the manybody problem was shown to highlight the effects of communication overloads. This chapter will illustrate how a parallel program can be written by improving on the sequential algorithm. Several numerical methods, used for solving different types of problems, will be parallelized in order to illustrate the basics of parallel programming.

8.1 How to get started

While coding any parallel program the following points should be kept in mind:

1. There should be equal allocation of input data to the different processors. This is to ensure that all the processors take more or less the same computation time.

2. The next thing that should be noted is that the computational work must be distributed judiciously to each processor, such that all of them have approximately the same workload.

3. The parallel program should not take up more time than the sequential program.

4. The coding of the program should be done judiciously to optimize interprocessor communication, since communication between the processors takes up a lot of time. Routines like `gathreal`, `gathint`, `scatint`, `scatany`, etc. take 1 tick for execution as they don't have to transfer only a few bytes of data. Fromany takes about 2 ticks to transfer up to 100 bytes on a four dimensional hypercube. For a two dimensional hypercube it takes 1 tick. The `fork` routine on the other hand, takes up a lot of overhead time. It takes a constant overhead time of 27 ticks for mask equal to two, three, and four, but it takes 31 ticks to fork for mask = 0, i.e in a sequential computer. The `forkall` routine, on the other hand, is dimension dependent. The time in ticks that the `forkall` routine takes to execute for different dimensions of the hypercube is tabulated in Table 8.1. Note that 182 ticks is equal to about 10 seconds.

Table 8.1 *Time to execute forkall for different dimensions of hypercube*

Dimension	No. of Ticks
0	0
1	27
2	53
3	80
4	106

8.2 Some elementary programs

There are several techniques for coding parallel programs. This section aims to get the reader acquainted with some of these techniques, to enable him to successfully write efficient programs on his own.

8.2.1 Fork and nodeid

To check the functions of the `fork` routine and the `nodeid` routine a very simple program can be written:

1. Fork to all the processors.

2. Check and print the node ID or binary label of each processor.

3. Terminate work on all the processors that the host processor had forked on to.

A listing of this program is given below.

```
/* Demo of forkall and Nodeid */
#include <parc2.h>
void main()
{
    int i;
    forkall();
    i = nodeid();
    printf("\n This is processor number %d\n",i);
    if(i) terminate();
}
```

Fig. 8.1 *Demonstration of forkall and nodeid*

8.2.2 Expression evaluation

The next simple example illustrates how a complicated expression can be broken up into small and simple expressions and solved in parallel. The expression to be evaluated is:

$$E = a_6/((a_7/a_1.a_2.a_3.a_4.a_5) + a_7/a_8). \tag{8.1}$$

This expression can be rewritten as:

$$\tilde{E} = ((-a_6/a_8.a_7/a_8)/(a_1.a_2.a_3.a_4.a_5 + a_7/a_8)) + a_6/a_8. \tag{8.2}$$

The above expression is known as the Winograd Algorithm. It can be solved in parallel by assigning each processor a specific task and then collecting the results from the different processors to evaluate the final answer in processor zero. A listing of this program is given in Fig. 8.2. One important point should be kept in mind during expression evaluation. Evaluation of a small expression consumes more time when executed in parallel due to large communication overheads. Thus, unless the expression is very large, involving a large amount of data, it is not economical to solve them using a parallel machine. But one can practice coding such a program, just to get acquainted with parallel programming.

```
/* expression evaluation */
#include<parc2.h>
main()
{
int nid,i,st_time,end_time;
float exp,a[10], r1,r2,pdt;
printf("\nvalues of a1 to a8 :\n");
```

```
for(i=0;i<8;++i)
    scanf("%f",&a[i]);
st_time=timetick();
fork(1);
fork(2);
st_time=timetick();
nid=nodeid();
if(nid==1)
{
    pdt=1.0;
    for(i=0;i<5;++i)
        pdt*=a[i];
}
fromany2((char far *)&pdt,4,1);
if(nid==2)
    r1=a[6]/a[7];
fromany2((char far *)&r1,4,2);
if(nid==3)
    r2=a[5]/a[7];
fromany2((char far *)&r2,4,3);
if(!nid)
{
    exp = ((-1)*r1*r2)/(pdt+r1);
    exp += r2;
    printf("\nvalue of the expression :\n");
    printf(" %f\n",exp);
    end_time=timetick();
    printf("\ntime = %u\n",end_time - st_time);
}
else
    terminate();
}
```

Fig. 8.2 *Expression evaluation*

8.2.3 Matrix addition

Matrix addition is the simplest matrix operation. For two matrices to be added, they should have the same number of rows and columns. The matrix addition given in Fig. 8.3 is for matrices with three rows and any number of columns. The two matrices get copied to all the three links when the fork routine is called twice, once with mask 1 and then with mask 2. Then matrix addition for one row is carried out in each of the three processors in parallel. For example, processor one adds the elements of the first rows of the two matrices and stores them in the first row of another matrix. Then the rows of the matrix containing the sum are broadcast to all the other nodes. The final matrix is printed in processor zero.

```c
/* addition of 3 X m matrices */
#include<parc2.h>
main()
{
int i,nid,j,n,np,a[3][3],b[3][3],c[3][3];
printf("\nenter no. of columns of matrix a & b\n");
scanf("%d",&n);
printf("\nmatrix a\n");
for(i=0;i<3;++i)
{
    for(j=0;j<n;++j)
    {
        scanf("%d",&a[i][j]);
    }
}
printf("\nmatrix b\n");
for(i=0;i<3;++i)
{
    for(j=0;j<n;++j)
    {
        scanf("%d",&b[i][j]);
    }
}
fork(1);
fork(2);
nid=nodeid();
if(!nid)
{
    for(j=0;j<n;++j)
        c[0][j]=a[0][j]+b[0][j];
}
if(nid)
{
    for(j=0;j<n;++j)
        c[nid][j]=a[nid][j]+b[nid][j];
}
if(!nid)
for(i=1;i<=3;i++)
    fromany2((char far *)c[i],(n*2),i);
if(!nid)
{
    printf("\nmatrix c\n");
```

```
        for(i=0;i<=2;++i)
        {
            printf("\n");
            for(j=0;j<n;++j)
                printf(" %d ",c[i][j]);
        }
}
terminate();
}
```

Fig. 8.3 *Matrix addition*

8.2.4 Matrix multiplication

Matrix multiplication is one of the most important matrix operations. Two matrices can be multiplied if, and only if, the number of columns of the first matrix is equal to the number of rows of the second matrix. Another important thing to note is that matrix multiplication is not commutative.

A parallel program for the multiplication of two matrices is given in Fig. 8.4. Each row operation is carried out in a different processor. The results of each row operation is broadcast to all the other processors that are forked in. The final result is printed in the zeroth processor.

```
forkall();
clrscr();
nid = nodeid();
np = numproc();
/* compute the block size for all processors */
blk = N / np;
bsize = blk * sizeof(int) * N;
k1 = nid * blk;
/* compute row wise */
if (nid == (np - 1))
    M = N;
else
    M = (nid + 1) * blk;
for(l = k1; l < M ; l ++)
    for(i = 0; i < N; i++)
    {
        for(j = 0; j < N; j++)
        {
            C[l][i] += A[l][j]*B[j][i];
        }
        printf(" C[%d][%d] = %d ",l,i,C[l][i]);
    }
```

```
if (np > 1)
    for(index= 0; index < np; index++)
        fromany((char *)&C[index*blk][0], bsize, index);
```

Fig. 8.4 *Matrix multiplication body*

8.2.5 Linear curve fit

The method of *least squares* is one of the most systematic procedures to fit a unique curve through a given set of points and is widely used in practical computations. It can easily be implemented on a digital computer.

Let (x_i, y_i), $i \in [1, \ldots, n]$ be a set of data points, and let the given curve be $y = f(x)$. The error obtained on approximating x by x_i and y by y_i at each point is

$$e_i = y_i - f(x_i). \tag{8.3}$$

The total error associated with the total data set can be expressed as the sum of the squares of the errors at each point. If S is the sum of the squares of the errors, then

$$S = (y_1 - f(x_1))^2 + (y_2 - f(x_2))^2 + \ldots + (y_n - f(x_n))^2, \tag{8.4}$$

i.e

$$S = e_1^2 + e_2^2 + \ldots + e_n^2. \tag{8.5}$$

The method of least squares consists of minimizing S. The programs are given as Figs. 8.5 and 8.6. In these programs, a straight line $y = a_0 + a_1 x$ was fitted to a set of data using the method of least squares. Without going into the details of the steps involved in minimizing S, the two final expressions that were obtained are given below:

$$na_0 + a_1 \sum_{i=1}^{n} x_i = \sum_{i=1}^{n} y_i, \tag{8.6}$$

and

$$a_0 \sum_{i=1}^{n} x_i + a_1 \sum_{i=1}^{n} x_i^2 = \sum_{i=1}^{n} x_i y_i, \tag{8.7}$$

a_0 and a_1 were obtained by solving these two simultaneous equations in parallel. In this case also, the parallel program was less time-consuming only when the total number of elements in the data set was very large. For small data sets, the sequential program was faster.

```c
/* The following is the first half of the curve fitting
program. Method of least square fit  for linear eqn. */
#include<parc2.h>
main()
{
float x[20],y[20],xsm,xqsm,xysm,a0,a1,ysm,osum,tsum,den;
int i,nid,n;
printf("\ntotal no. of points");
scanf("%d",&n);
printf("\narray x");
for(i=0;i<n;++i)
    scanf("%f",&x[i]);
printf("\narray y");
for(i=0;i<n;++i)
    scanf("%f",&y[i]);
fork(1);
fork(2);
nid=nodeid();
if(!nid)
{
    ysm=0.0;
    for(i=0;i<n;++i)
        ysm+=y[i];
}
if(!nid)
    printf("\nscatany2...\n");
scatany2((int *)&ysm,4);
if(nid==1)
{
    xsm=0;
    for(i=0;i<n;++i)
        xsm+=x[i];
}
if(nid==2)
{
    xqsm=0;
    for(i=0;i<n;++i)
        xqsm+=(x[i]*x[i]);
}
if(nid==3)
{
    xysm=0;
    for(i=0;i<n;++i)
        xysm+=(x[i]*y[i]);
}
fromany2((char far *)&xsm,4,1);
```

```
fromany2((char far *)&xqsm,4,2);
fromany2((char far *)&xysm,4,3);
```

Fig. 8.5 *First half of the curve-fit program*

```
if(nid)
{
    switch(nid)
    {
        case 1:
            osum=(xqsm*ysm)-(xsm*xysm);
            break;
        case 2:
            tsum=(n*xysm)-(xsm*ysm);
            break;
        case 3:
            den=(n*xqsm)-(xsm*xsm);
            break;
    }
}
fromany2((char far *)&osum,4,1);
fromany2((char far *)&tsum,4,2);
fromany2((char far *)&den,4,3);
if(!nid)
{
    a0=((double) osum)/((double) den);
    a1=((double) tsum)/((double) den);
    printf("\nthe fit : \n");
    printf("\n Y =   %f + %f x\n",a0,a1);
}
else    terminate();
}
```

Fig. 8.6 *Second half of the curve-fit program*

8.2.6 Gaussian elimination

Gaussian elimination is a method for solving a system of linear equations. Consider a system of n linear equations containing m variables.

$$\begin{aligned}
a_{11}x_1 + a_{12}x_2 + \ldots + a_{1m}x_m &= b_1 \\
a_{21}x_1 + a_{22}x_2 + \ldots + a_{2m}x_m &= b_2 \\
&\vdots \\
a_{n1}x_1 + a_{n2}x_2 + \ldots + a_{nm}x_m &= b_n.
\end{aligned} \quad (8.8)$$

Case Studies 83

It is assumed that the system of equations is consistent. An augmented matrix of the system is formed:

$$\begin{pmatrix} a_{11} & a_{12} & \ldots & a_{1m} & b_1 \\ a_{21} & a_{22} & \ldots & a_{2m} & b_2 \\ \ldots & \ldots & \ldots & \ldots & \ldots \\ a_{n1} & a_{n2} & \ldots & a_{nm} & b_n \end{pmatrix}. \qquad (8.9)$$

In the next step, the matrix is upper triangularized using the usual method of matrix triangularization. Backtracking is done on the upper triangularized matrix to obtain the solution set.

In the parallel program, as given in Figs. 8.7 and 8.8, each row was assigned to a different processor which carried out the different operations in parallel. After each operation was executed, the results of each row were broadcast to all the other processors, to enable them to start the next set of operations.

```
/* upper triangularization */
forkall();
st_tm=timetick();
nid=nodeid();
if(!nid)
{
    for(col=0;col<=m;++col)
        u[0][col]=a[0][col];
}
for(k=0;k<n-1;++k)
{
    if(nid>k)
    {
        for(col=0;col<=m;++col)
        {
            if(a[k][k]!=0)
                u[nid][col]=a[nid][col]-(a[nid][k]*a[k][col])/a[k][k];
        }
    }
    for(i=1;i<=n;++i)
        fromany((char far *)u[i],(4*(m+1)),i);
    for(i=k+1;i<n;++i)
    {
        for(j=0;j<=m;++j)
        {
            a[i][j]=u[i][j];
        }
    }
}
```

Fig. 8.7 *Triangularization*

```
/* backtracking */
x[n-1]=a[n-1][m]/a[n-1][n-1];
for(k=n-2;k>=0;--k)
{
    sum=0.0;
    for(i=n-1;i>=k;--i)
        sum+=u[k][i]*x[i];
    x[k]=(u[k][m]-sum)/u[k][k];
}
```

Fig. 8.8 *Back-substitution*

8.2.7 Simpson's 1/3rd rule

The Simpson's 1/3rd Rule is an important rule for solving definite integrals numerically. In this rule, the whole interval should be divided into an even number of subintervals, each of the same width h. Without going into the details of the derivation of the formula, the Simpson's 1/3rd rule can be stated as follows

$$\int_{x_0}^{x_n} ydx = \frac{h}{3}(y_0 + 4(y_1 + y_3 + \ldots + y_{n-1})$$

$$+ 2(y_2 + y_4 + \ldots + y_{n-2}) + y_n) \qquad (8.10)$$

A listing of this method, executed in parallel, is given in Fig. 8.9. Parallelism is achieved by first dividing the total interval into an even number of subintervals, then each processor is made to calculate the value of the function in a particular subinterval. The value of the function in all the subintervals is then gathered and summed up in processor zero.

```
forkall();
nid=nodeid();
np=numproc();
h=(u-1)/(10.0*np);      /* stepsize */
if(!nid)
{
    for(i=0;i<10;++i)
        ysm=f((1+(i*h)));
}
if(nid)
{
    for(i=0;i<10;++i)
        ysm=f(nid*(h*i));
        if((nid*h)!=1 && (nid*h)!=u)
```

```
            {
                if((nid%2)==0)
                    ysm*=2;
                if((nid%2)!=0)
                    ysm*=4;
            }
    }
    gathreal(ysm,&sum);
    if(!nid)
    {
        sum=(h/3)*sum;
        printf("\nvalue of the integral = %f\n",sum);
    }
    else
        terminate();
}
```

Fig. 8.9 Simpson's 1/3rd rule

8.2.8 Filon's formula

Filon, in 1928, derived a set of formulae for computing *Fourier integrals*. These integrals involve oscillatory functions and are of the form:

$$I_c = \int_a^b f(x) \cos(\omega x) dx, \tag{8.11}$$

or

$$I_s = \int_a^b f(x) \sin(\omega x) dx, \tag{8.12}$$

which are known as *Fourier integrals*. They occur in practical applications, such as *spectral analysis*.

In Filon's method, the interval $[a, b]$ was divided into $2N$ subintervals and, in each double interval, $f(x)$ is approximated by a quadratic. This rule is similar to the Simpson's rule stated above, except that there is a factor $\cos(\omega x)$ in the first equation and a factor $\sin(\omega x)$ in the second equation. The first equation was solved in parallel. The steps for solving are given below

1. $h = (b-a)/2N$

2. Let $c_1 = 1/2 f(a) \cos(\omega a) + f(a+2h) \cos(\omega(a+2h)) + \ldots + 1/2 f(b) \cos(\omega b)$,

3. Let $c_2 = f(a+h)\cos(\omega(a+h)) + f(a+3h)\cos(\omega(a+3h)) + \ldots + f(b-h)\cos(\omega(b-h))$.

4. Then, $I_c = h[\alpha f(b)\sin(\omega b) - f(a)\sin(\omega a)] + \beta c_1 + \delta c_2$,

where

$$\alpha = (\omega^2 h^2 + \omega h \sin(\omega h)\cos(\omega h) - 2\sin^2(\omega h))/\omega^3 h^3, \qquad (8.13)$$

$$\beta = 2[\omega h(1 + \cos^2(\omega h)) - 2\sin(\omega h]/\omega^3 h^3, \qquad (8.14)$$

$$\delta = 4(\sin(\omega h) - \omega h \cos(\omega h))/\omega^3 h^3. \qquad (8.15)$$

A listing of the parallel program is given in Fig. 8.10. At first the `fork` routine is executed with mask equal to one and two. Then, c_1 and c_2 are calculated in parallel and the results are broadcast to all the processors that have been forked. Next α, β, and δ are also calculated and the results are scattered to all the processors that are active. The final evaluation of I_c is done in processor zero.

```
forkall();
nid=nodeid();
np=numproc();
h=(u-1)/(2.0*np);
if(nid)
{
 sm1=f(1+(2.0*nid*h))*cos(w*(1+(2.0*nid*h)));
 sm2=f(1+(((2.0*nid)-1.0)*h))*cos(w*(((2.0*nid)-1.0)*h));
    if((nid*h*2.0)==u)
    {
        sm1/=2.0;
        sm2=0.0;
    }
}
gathreal(sm1, &c1);
gathreal(sm2, &c2);
c1+=(f(1)*cos(w*1))/2.0;
c2+=f(1+h)*cos(w*(1+h));
if(nid==1)
{
    a=1.0/(w*h);
    b=2.0/((pow(w,2))*(pow(h,2)));
    d=(4.0*sin(w*h))/((pow(w,3))*(pow(h,3)));
}
if(nid==2)
{
```

```
      a=sin(2.0*w*h)/(2.0*(pow(w,2))*(pow(h,2)));
      b=((pow(cos(w*h),2))*2.0)/((pow(w,3))*(pow(h,3)));
      d=(4.0*cos(w*h))/((pow(w,2))*(pow(h,2)));
}
if(nid==3)
{
      a=(2*(pow(sin(w*h),2)))/((pow(w,3))*(pow(h,3)));
      b=((-1)*2*sin(2*w*h))/((pow(w,3))*(pow(h,3)));
}
if(nid!=1 && nid!=2 && nid!=3)
{
      a=0.0;
      b=0.0;
      d=0.0;
}
gathreal(a,&alpha);
gathreal(b,&beta);
gathreal(d,&delta);
if(!nid)
{
I=h*(alpha*((f(u)*sin(w*u))-
(f(l)*sin(w*l)))+(beta*c1)+(delta*c2));
printf("\nvalue of the integral = %f \n",I);
}
else
terminate();
```

Fig. 8.10 *Fourier integral by Filon's method*

8.3 Exercises

1. Write a dimension-independent C program to perform LU-decomposition and back-substitution on a square matrix.

2. Write a dimension-independent C program to compute the eigenvalues of a square matrix.

3. Write a routine that scatters a two-dimensional matrix from a node with label 0 to all other nodes.

4. Write a routine that updates the jth row of a $M \times N$ matrix, each of whose elements is $size$ bytes long, with the original coming from the jth row of the ith node.

Bibliography

[1] Flynn, M.J., Some Computer Organizations and their Effectiveness, *IEEE Trans Comput*, **21**(9):948–960

[2] Backus, J. (Aug 1978), Can Programming be Liberated from the von Neumann Style? — A Functional Style and its Algebra of Programs, *Comm. of the ACM*, **21**(8): 613–641.

[3] Hwang, K. (1993), *Advanced Computer Architecture: Parallelism, Scalability and Programmability*, McGraw Hill.

[4] Dally, W.J. (April, 1992), Fiske, J., Keen, J., Lethin, R., Noakes, M., Nuth, P. Davison, R. and Fyler, G., The Message-Driven Processor: A Multicomputer Processing Node with Efficient Mechanisms, *IEEE Micro*, **12**(2):23–29.

[5] Karp, A.H. and Babb, R.G. (September, 1988), A Comparison of 12 Parallel Fortran Dialects, *IEEE Software*, 52–66.

[6] "Microprocessors", Order Number 230843-007, Intel Corporation Literature Sales Department, P.O. Box 7641, Mt. Prospect IL 60056-7641.

[7] Sastri, V. (March, 1996), What is New in Computers — Intel's New P6 Processor, *Resonance*, **1**(3):96–102.

[8] Treibel, W.A. and Singh, A. (1995), *The 8088 and 8086 Microprocessors — Programming, Interfacing, Software, Hardware and Applications*, Prentice Hall of India Pvt. Ltd.

[9] Hamacher, V.C., Vranesic, Z. and Zaky, S. (1991), *Computer Organization*, McGraw-Hill.

[10] Patterson and Hennessey (1990), *Computer Organization*, McGraw-Hill.

[11] *Microprocessors and Peripheral Handbook—Volume* **2**:*Peripherals*,

Order Number 230843-005, Intel Corporation Literature Distribution, Mail Stop SC6-59, 3065 Bowers Avenue, Santa Clara, CA 95051.

[12] "ASM86 Assembly Language Reference Manual", Order Number 122385-001, Intel Corporation Literature Sales Department, P.O. Box 7641, Mt. Prospect IL 60056-7641.

[13] "Turbo Assembler User Guide", Borland International, 1800 Green Hills Road, P. O. Box 660 001, Scotts Valley CA 95066-0001.

[14] Norton, P. and Socha, J. (1989), *Peter Norton's Assembly Language Programming Book for the IBM PC*, Prentice Hall of India.

[15] "PC/XT Technical Reference Manual", IBM Corporation, Boca Raton, 1984.

[16] "PC/AT Technical Reference Manual", IBM Corporation, Boca Raton, 1985.

[17] Norton, P. (1993), *Inside the IBM PC*, Fourth Edition, Prentice Hall of India.

[18] Duncan, R. (1986), *Advanced MSDOS Programming*, Microsoft Press.

[19] Mueller, S. (1994), *Upgrading and Repairing PCs*, Fourth Edition, Prentice Hall, India.

[20] *Que's MSDOS-5 User's Guide* (1993), Special Edition, Prentice Hall of India.

[21] *The MSDOS Encyclopedia* (1988), Microsoft Press.

[22] Ghoshal, S.K. (February, 1996), The Personal Computer Hardware, *Resonance*, **1**(2):32–39.

[23] Ghoshal, S.K., and Kalai Selvi, S., MUSIX — A Simple Microkernel for Parallel Computing in Unix, *Proceedings of the Southern Regional Convention - 94, June 27–30*, Hyderabad, 65–71.

[24] "Intel 80386 Programmers' Reference Manual", Intel Corporation, Order Number 230985.

[25] "Intel 80386 System Software Writers' Guide", Intel Corporation, Order Number 231499.

[26] Ghoshal, S. K., Kalai Selvi, S., Youren, Z. and Nagendra Prasad, P. S., A Multimode Operating System for Distributed Computing in MSDOS, *Proceedings of the Southern Regional Convention - 94, June 27–30*, Hyderabad, 19–25.

[27] Nanda Kishore, D. and Ghoshal, S.K. (May–June 1996), Design, Programming Environment and Applications of a Simple Low-cost Message Passing Multicomputer, *Journal of the Indian Institute of Science*, **76**:337–361.

[28] Ghoshal, S.K., A Paradigm for Writing Scalable Programs on Message Passing Parallel Computers, *Current Trends in Advanced Computing — Proceedings of ADCOMP-95*: 164–169.

[29] *LSI Data Book* (1986), Monolithic Memories Inc., 2175 Mission College Boulevard, Santa Clara, CA 95054-1592.

[30] Maurice J. Bach (1988), *The Design of the Unix Operating System*, Prentice Hall of India.

[31] dma.c and the routines handling DMA in the Unix Source Code, Unix System V/386, Source Code Provision Release Notes, 1988, AT & T Customer Information Centre, Customer Service Representative, P. O. Box 19901, Indianapolis, Indiana 46219, USA.

[32] Linux Source code from http://www.linux.org/

[33] Linux Source code from http://www.redhat.com/

[34] Linux Source code from http://sunsite.unc.edu/

[35] Chhabra, S. (1991), A DMA-based Interprocessor Communication Interface for Parallel Computing, M.E. Project Report, Department of Computer Science and Automation, Indian Institute of Science, Bangalore.

[36] Ghoshal, S.K., Guha, S., Ariff, S.M. and Rajaraman, V. (1990), Simple Low-cost Multiprocessor Based on Message Passing FIFO Links, *Microprocessors and Microsystems*, **14**:297–300, Butterworth Scientific Ltd., Guildford, Surrey, UK.

[37] Suryanarayan, P. and Ghoshal, S. K., Synthesis of Parallel Programs for Message Passing Multicomputers, *Proceedings of the Southern Regional Convention - 94*, June 27–30, Hyderabad:1–6.

[38] SCO Unix Operating System User's Reference Manual (1993), The Santa Cruz Operation Inc., 400 Encinal Street, Santa Cruz, CA 95060, USA.

[39] Ghoshal S.K. (1988), The Numerical Integration of Ordinary Differential Equations on Multiprocessing Systems, Ph. D. Thesis, Department of Computer Science and Automation, Indian Institute of Science, Bangalore.

[40] Hoare, C.A.R. (1987), *Communicating Sequential Processes*, Prentice Hall.

[41] *CMOS parallel First-in/First-out FIFO* (Feb. 1986), Data sheet, Integrated Device Technology, Inc.

[42] Brown S.D., Francis R.J. and Vranesic Z.G. (1992), *Field Programmable Gate Arrays*, Kluwer Academic Publishers, Assinpi Park, Massachusetts.

[43] *The Programmable Gate Array Data Book* (1994), Xilinx Inc., 2100 Logic Drive, San Jose, California 95124.

[44] Ghoshal, S.K. (April 1996), "Know your Personal Computer - 3. The Personal Computer System Software", *Resonance*, **1**(4):31–36.

[45] Ghoshal S.K. and Pathak D. Modeling of an Interoperable Parallel File System, accepted in *ADCOMP-96*.

[46] Fox, G., Johnson, M., Lyzenga, G., Otto, S., Salmon, J. and Walker, D. (1988), *Solving Problems on Concurrent Processors, Volume 1 — General Techniques and Regular Problems*, Prentice Hall.

[47] "Multibus II Bus Architecture Specification Handbook", Order Number 146077, Intel Corporation Literature Sales Department, P.O. Box 7641, Mt. Prospect IL 60056-7641.

[48] "64-bit VMEbus Specification" (January, 1990), VME Bus International Trade Association and IEEE P1014 Working Group.

[49] "iLBX II Backplane User's guide", Order Number 146709-001, Intel Corporation Literature Sales Department, P.O. Box 7641, Mt. Prospect IL 60056-7641.

[50] "Message-passing Coprocessor User Manual", Order Number 176526-001, Intel Corporation Literature Sales Department, P.O. Box 7641, Mt. Prospect IL 60056-7641.

[51] "Message-passing Coprocessor Data Sheet", Order Number 290145-002, Intel Corporation Literature Sales Department.

[52] Richard Stevens (1996), *Unix Network Programming*, Prentice-Hall of India Private Limited.

[53] Patterson and Hennessy (1990), *Computer Architecture — A Quantitative Approach*, Morgan Kaufmann.

[54] *Core: Concurrent Runtime Environment on Paras 8600 for C users* (February, 1994), Centre for Development of Advanced Computing, 2/1 Brunton Road, Bangalore 560 025, India.

[55] IMS T800 Transputer Electrical Databook (April, 1987), INMOS Limited, 1000 Aztec West, Almondsbury, Bristol BS12 4SQ England.

[56] Kung S.Y. (1988), *VLSI Array Processors*, Prentice Hall International, Englewood Cliffs, NJ, USA.

[57] Laxmivarahan, M.A. and Dhall, S. (1990), *Analysis and Design of Parallel Algorithms — Arithmetic and Matrix Problems*, McGraw Hill.

[N_1] A. Geist, A. Beguelin, Jack Dongarra, W. Jiang, R. Manchek and V. Sunderam, *PVM: Parallel Virtual Machine — A Users Guide and Tutorial for Networked Parallel Computing*, The MIT Press, Cambridge, Massachusetts.

[N_2] *Online PVM source code and documentation from* 144.16.67.161 *by anonymous ftp*. Get /docs/pvm/README.

[N_3] *IBM Parallel Environment for AIX: MPI Programming and Subroutine Reference, Version 2, Release 1*, IBM Corporation, Department 55JA, Mail Station P384, 522 South Bend Road, Poughkeepsie, NY, 12601-5400, USA.

[N_4] *Online MPI source code and documentation from* 144.16.67.161 *by anonymous ftp*. Get /tools/MPI/README.txt.

Index of terms

A20 Gating, 28
architectural features of FIFO card, 37
assembly language programming, 26
a symmetric usage of low-level functions, 61

back-end processor, 21
backplane, 15–17, 20
BIOS, 26, 46, 49
block diagram of FIFO card, 35
board-level architecture, 26
Bread function, 57–58
Bwrite function, 58
bus
  single, 5
  multiple, 5
C language, 56–57
case studies of parallelizing applications, 74–75
challenge of building parallel computer, 47–48
CISC, 19–20
CMOS checksum, 48–49
CMOS-RAM, 17
coarse-grained task-partitioning, 18–19
compilers, 16–18, 26–29
computation of π, 69
CPU, 3–4, 15–20, 22–23, 25–27, 31, 36, 39–41, 54–55
crossbar switches, 6

CSP, 32, 71
curve-fitting, 80–82

data parallelism, 2
decoder, 36
degree of parallelism, 2
degree of a node, 7
design consideration of DIPP, 40–51, 56
different approach for high-level programming, 65
dimension-independent parallel programming, 50
dimhyp function, 58–59
Diophantine-predicate satisfiability problem, 71–72
DMA, 15, 31, 41
driver routines for FIFO, 46, 49, 51

E^3-routing, 65–66
EGA (Enhanced Graphics Adaptor), 30
embedded microprocessors, 21
embedding, 12
EPROM, 32, 36–40, 46–49, 56–60
equivalent of POST in SERC firmware, 60–61
ethernet, 20, 55
expression evaluation, 76–77

FDDI, 20
FIFO card, 34–42

FIFO chip, 32, 34, 37–38, 40–42
Filon's formulae, 85–86
fine-grained task-partitioning, 21–22
flushing FIFO link, 48
Flynn's taxonomy, 2–4
Fork function usage example, 75–76
Fork function description, 56–57
forkall function description, 61–62
FORTRAN, 28, 50
Fourier integrals, 85
fromany function description, 64
front-end processor, 21

gather functions, 63
Gaussian elimination, 82–83
getting started on our machine, 74–75

hardware parallelism, 2
high-level language (HLL), 2, 18, 20, 26, 28, 49, 56, 61
high-level library, 50
Hops, 12
hierarchical design of system software, 45–46
hypercubes, 11–13

IDT 7203 FIFO chip, 32, 34
image recognition, 72
initialization of FIFO links, 47–49
instruction-level parallelism, 18
interconnection networks
   dynamic, 5–6
   static, 7–11

job-level parallelism, 18

limitations of SERC firmware, 49–50
linear curve fitting, 81
LED, 37, 39
linear array, 2, 7–8
link between two nodes, 36

loosely coupled system, 3–4

manybody problem, 69–71
marshalling, 54
master, 5–6, 16, 46, 47, 57
matrix addition, 77–78
matrix multiplication, 79–80
memory management units (MMUs), 16–17
mesh, 9–10, 12
microkernel, 28, 50
microtasking switch, 18
MISD, 2–3
MIMD, 3
microprocessor(s), 25–26
motherboard(s), 26–27
multibus, 15–16
multicasting, 39, 46
multistage interconnecting networks (MIN), 5–6
multicomputer(s), 3–4, 7, 19–22
multilayered PCBs, 42
multiprocessor(s), 3–4, 9, 18–19, 50–51, 60, 65, 68

need to change SERC firmware, 49
need to maintain symmetry, 60
NMI, 36
nodeid function, 59–60
nodeid usage example, 75–76
numpro function, 62

open systems, 44–45

PAL, 30, 36–38, 40, 42
parallel computing, 1, 25, 31, 68
Pascal, 28, 50, 70, 72
philosophy of DIPP, 49–51, 56, 65
POST, 36
POST – counterpart in SERC firmware, 60–61
Prolog, 28, 50, 71–72

read-before-write hazard, 23
re-invoking POST, 49
ring, 8

RISC, 19–20

scatter functions, 63
set motherboard configuration, 27
shared memory, 15–18, 23, 29–30
Simpson's 1/3rd rule, 84–85
SISD, 2
SIMD, 3
slaves, 5, 46–47
software parallelism, 2
specifications of DIPP, 50–51
star, 9
status ports, 32, 41
subroutine-level parallelism, 18
SVGA (Super VGA), 30

termall function, 62
terminate function, 59–60

tightly coupled system, 3
temporal parallelism, 2
topologies
 symmetric, 4
 asymmetric, 4
torus, 10
transputer, 22
tree, 8–9

Unix, 17, 21, 27–28, 31, 50

VGA (Versatile Graphics Array)
 adaptor, 30
video-RAM, 30
VLSI, 20, 22
von Neumann bottleneck, 3

write-after-write hazard, 23